Boomers at Work

Boomers at Work

Re/Working Retirement

Sandra Konrad

Cover design: Marianne Unger, Mudstudio, Victoria
Illustrations and author photo: Laura Kennedy

All rights reserved. This book, or parts thereof, may not be reproduced in any form without permission from the publisher; exceptions are made for brief excerpts used in published reviews.

A few people interviewed for this book granted permission to use their full name. Many gave permission to use their first name. Several requested a pseudonym with their identifying information altered.

Care has been taken to trace ownership of copyright material contained and credited in this book. However, the author welcomes information that enables correction of any reference or credit in subsequent editions.

Every effort has been made to provide accurate, up-to-date information. The ideas expressed are those of the author. This book is sold with the understanding that the publisher is not engaged in rendering professional advice. If expert assistance is required, the services of a competent professional should be sought.

Library and Archives Canada Cataloguing in Publication
Copyright © 2017 Sandra Konrad
Konrad, Sandra J., author
Boomers at work : re/working retirement / Sandra Konrad.

Includes bibliographical references.
ISBN 9781542484800 (softcover)

1. Baby boom generation--Employment--Canada. 2. Retirees--Employment--Canada. 3. Older people--Employment--Canada. 4. Age and employment--Canada. 5. Older people--Canada. 6. Work--Psychological aspects. 7. Retirement--Psychological aspects. I. Title.

HD6283.C3K66 2017   331.3'980971   C2017-900912-5
ISBN: 1542484804
Printed in the United States of America

Boomers at Work: Re/Working Retirement

Salutes the

Front-end baby boomers

Who are

Building a long career path

Contents

One	Boomers Build a Long Career Path	1
Two	Boomers and the New Look of Work	4
Three	Show Me the Money	14
Four	Sixty Is the New…Sixty	35
Five	The Roof over Our Heads	51
Six	Re/Working Retirement	68
Seven	Working for the Good Life	87
Eight	Older Workers at Work	97
Nine	Bringing Experience to Work	120
Ten	Our Dreams for Our Sixties	136
Eleven	Channel Your Inner Worker	145
Twelve	We Build Our Career Path as We Travel	154
Epilogue	What Are They Doing Now?	161
Acknowledgements		167
Appendix	Keeping Older Workers at Work: Hard Policies and Soft Programs	169
Resources		171

The good life is a process,

not a state of being.

It is a journey,

not a destination.

CARL ROGERS

One

Boomers Build a Long Career Path

Around the time I turned 58 I changed my career focus and then shortly after discovered two things: the road sign pointed only toward work, and I didn't have a map. I couldn't see even much of a road. I had no idea where I was going, but I deduced I'd be on the road a long time.

Until then I had assumed that my career path was leading straight to retirement. But no. I wasn't going to have enough money to retire and do the things I still hoped to do. I didn't have a pension, and twice, my savings had been deeply cut by market "corrections." Too, I'd quit saving for retirement during a long spell of poor health and hadn't been able to work full-time after I went back.

I set out on the traditional education-work-retirement life path when I started my first job at 21, believing in its inviolability. The future was rosy for front-end boomers, born between 1946 and 1954. We had no trouble getting jobs with generous benefits and could pencil 'retirement' into a future calendar. Now, if retirement was what I should be doing next but I wasn't going to retire, then something was wrong. I was in shock.

I've known for a long time that front-end boomers—my age-mates—had experienced similar life events, and that our lives had turned out differently than those of our parents. More of us finished high school and graduated with a post-secondary education than they did; we married at a later age, had few children and had them later, and made divorce commonplace. Men and increasingly women went to work and developed a new approach to work: career mobility. We paid into Canada's pension plan, bought RRSPs and expected to retire at 65. But retirement was too far in the future to give it much attention.

I became curious about my age-mates. If I was facing this unexpected challenge, were they, too? Then, in the early 2010s the news media began airing stories that boomers had nowhere near enough money to retire; a bit later, they said that boomers might work beyond the usual retirement age.

What were boomers doing? How had their careers developed? Had they experienced glitches in their life and careers that were pushing them to keep working, as I had? How did they view retirement? When were they going to retire? (Retiring from a first career and taking a second or encore career was a recent phenomenon).

I set out to answer those questions and to write about what I found.

The first thing I needed to do was to ask Canadian boomers, who planned to work past 65 and likely until 70, for their answers. During the course of locating and interviewing people from across the country, I discovered that many had eliminated the notion of age as a criterion for retirement. Instead, they thought of retirement as driven by the state of their health, by their desire to work, or by their wish to engage in activities other than work.

I had intended to talk only to those who had not yet retired, thinking the differences between those who had to work and those who wanted to work were great. Before long I learned that there are few differences between people who had retired from one career and started a second or even third career, and those who wouldn't retire in the traditional sense. My friends and colleagues were willing to pass on my request for interviews to their friends, in an ever-growing circle. The response from an ad in *Zoomer* magazine brought several willing participants. In the end, forty people told me about their choices and careers, even aspects of their life stories I had assumed might be hard to tell a stranger. I've used the actual first names and identifying information of most of the people, but a few asked me to use a pseudonym and altered identifying information.

Money is one of the major reasons we'll work. Many of us don't have a work-place pension, nor will the Canada and Quebec Pension Plans and

Old Age Security provide an adequate post-work income. Many haven't saved enough for retirement, and it's unlikely we'll develop a strong savings habit at this late date. But, there are other reasons we're extending our careers into our late sixties and even seventies, reasons we couldn't have anticipated 40 years ago, when we first began to work.

This book sets out to describe why boomers are working, and how they want work to serve them now. People's opinions and actions vary and often contradict each other. Those contradictions show the diverse and rich ways boomers are building a longer career while they design a new way to work in their sixties and beyond.

We boomers have affected much social change simply because there are so many of us. We've charted many a new course. But a new course comes without road maps. Now, we are setting off to cross an undiscovered territory without a compass and intimate knowledge of the land. This book hopes to draw a rough map—though the road is under construction—by presenting the stories of Canadian boomers (our circumstances are different than our U.S. neighbours) who are charting a new career path.

I hope this book helps you to appreciate your needs to work, whatever those needs may be, and that it inspires you to find work that satisfies you. In most chapters I suggest activities to help you clarify your position on work, finances and retirement. Some exercises can take a while to complete; I suggest you use paper and pencil to scribble down your thoughts. Not all the activities will appeal or apply to you. Do those that intrigue you, in whatever order you like. If you find yourself resisting an activity, perhaps that's an indication of its importance to you. The first six areas of activities provide background information that will be helpful as you do *Plan Your Work Future* and *Set Goals*. You may want to discuss the questions and exercises as a couple or with friends.

"The best effect of any book," said Thomas Carlyle, "is that it excites the reader to self-activity." I hope that if you find yourself wondering about the future and are unsure of what work-leisure-money combination lies ahead, that *Boomers at Work* will help you see more options and choose work that suits you.

Two

Boomers and the New Look of Work

"Are you retired yet?" That's the usual opener at a party where most of the people appear to be 60 or older. It puts you on the spot.

We front-end boomers, born between 1946 and 1954, are struggling to answer that very question. The Silent Generation born, between 1925 and 1945, would have answered, "Yes, I'm retired" or said something about winding down their career and retiring soon. But as front-end boomers face one of life's significant transitions—from career to retirement—we're weighing an additional option, continuing to work and delaying retirement. Many of us want to keep working. Many have to. While we're deciding when and if we'll retire, retirement as a dependable life stage is changing.

I presume you have this book, Boomers at Work, in your hands because you're not sure whether to retire or keep working. Or do both.

Does one or more of these scenarios apply to you?

You're passionate about your work.

- You like working, and can't imagine what else could challenge and satisfy you the way work does.

- You want to try something new, work-wise. All along you've had the idea that one day you'd own your own business or indulge an artistic passion.
- You feel like your life won't be right if you don't pursue the career you gave up years ago.

You worry you'll feel bored or unfulfilled if you retire.

- You know that golfing or wintering in Arizona or Florida won't cut it in the big picture of your life.
- You've heard that happy retirees fill their time volunteering, but you're not inspired to volunteer.
- Your spouse isn't ready to quit work, and you'll be at loose ends if you're not working.
- You think retiring is what old people do—and you're not old.

Your finances won't allow you to retire.

- You don't have a workplace pension. Or, you can't access the pension you paid into in your home country.
- The latest increase on your cheque won't buy a cuppa joe at Tim's.
- Your income from CPP or QPP and OAS, even with the GIS—if you qualify—won't be nearly enough.
- You've saved enough money, but earning more will spice up retirement with travel or other interests.
- You've never earned enough to put money away for retirement.
- You were out of the workforce for several years, caring for children or recovering from a health crisis or job loss, and you need to build a nest-egg.
- You worry you'll outlive your retirement savings. But, who knows how much money you'll need and how long you'll live?
- Your RRSPs were decimated in recessions.
- You split your pension and assets 50-50 in divorce and now need to build savings again.

- You plan to live on your home equity, but you're not sure of the best way to do that.
- Your pension or retirement savings disappeared in a corporate bankruptcy, company raid of your pension fund, or Ponzi scheme.

If you said "That's me" to one or more of these scenarios, you're in good company. Many baby boomers won't be retiring any time soon, at least not fully. The lack of retirement savings is one of the biggest issues we face. The sharp downturn in the economy in 2016 created a sense of anxiety.

Who's Working?

Let's start with the numbers.

The number of Canadians 65 and older who participate in labour market activity has been increasing since 1996, says a 2010 Statistics Canada report.

- One in four Canadians aged 65 to 69 was in the labour force, in 2013.
- 6.7% of people 70 and older were in the labour force.
- The proportion of women in their eighties who were still working was similar to men.
- Seniors' participation rate in the labour force more than doubled, from six percent in 2000 to 13 percent in 2013, says a 2014 Government of Canada Action for Seniors report.
- In 2015, 9.5 percent of women 65 and older were in the workforce, up from eight percent 5 years earlier.
- Women aged 65 to 69 are the fastest growing segment of working seniors.

Men have always outnumbered women in the workforce across all age groups, but the gap between employed men and women over 55 is narrowing. In 2004, almost half of all women aged 55 to 64 were in the labour force. If not babysitting or caregiving, women have tended to work part-time; today, boomer women are three times more likely than men to work part-time.

Two out of three working men 65 and older were employed in consumer services, business services and primary industries such as farming, fishing, forestry and mining. Women have traditionally worked in consumer services as retail and sales clerks, and in business and health-related services. Today they are working in more diverse occupations.

Being in the labour force is associated with low and high incomes, more than middle incomes. It's also associated with higher education, which usually leads to less physically demanding work. Unskilled workers are less likely to work full-time, while people who are self-employed or have a management job more often work full-time. Finally, people who are still working tend to have a mortgage or are renting.

Why We're Working

Visions of working in our later years were already dancing in boomers' heads in 1999, the year AARP (formerly the American Association of Retired Persons) commissioned a study that asked 2001 U.S. boomers about their attitude toward retirement and their retirement savings behaviour. An astonishing 84 percent said they planned to work past the usual retirement age. Only 16 percent said they wouldn't work. Their answers clustered respondents into five groups.

- The *strugglers* who always needed every dollar they earned to live, and had never been able to save for retirement.
- The *anxious* who earned below average; they would work to supplement their scant savings, employer pensions and social security.
- The *self-reliants* who had earned enough to save aggressively for retirement, but planned to work at least part-time since they found work interesting, satisfying and challenging.
- The *traditionalists* who would need the money, but enjoyed work; this time around they'd start a business and work for themselves.
- The *enthusiasts,* that 16 percent, who were looking forward to retirement and had enough money to enjoy themselves, engaged in recreational activities.

Front-end Canadian boomers (the oldest turn 71 in 2017 and the youngest 63) are similar to our U.S. counterparts and plan to do much the same thing. We too have our enthusiasts who enjoy a leisured life, living on the pensions they began paying into 40-some years ago, but the majority of us plan to work. We haven't enough saved and need to supplement OAS and CPP, and only a third of Canadians have a pension from employment. As well, many want to start a business.

Recent recessions, with their job losses, lay-offs and stock market drops, are pushing many boomers to work a few more years. Although no one age group has lost jobs more than another, boomers will search for work longer than younger unemployeds, since we face an additional barrier to getting a job—stereotypes about older workers. We'll likely be the odd-person-out in the post-recessionary slow return to full-employment. Losing earning years, while we were building retirement nest-eggs, will force us to reduce our expectations of retirement or to push back our retirement age.

We have ridden waves of economic good and bad times in the last 40 years, with three recessions. Jobs have disappeared in industries such as the Atlantic fisheries, Silicon Valley North's tech sector, forestry in the west, funding cuts to healthcare, fluctuations in the price of oil, and in the manufacturing and auto industry in 2008-2009, when half a million jobs were lost.

We'll struggle to recover from the current downturn, with its long-term effects on our financial position. We'll encounter more booms, when fixed incomes and savings won't keep up with inflation, and more busts, when personal savings will fall. Continuing to earn and save, if possible, in our sixties and even seventies, can help us prepare for the future. Doing so can delay dipping into whatever savings we have, and reduce the inevitable struggle to make ends meet when the next downturn comes along.

What Work Means to You

Imagine a woman standing at a stove, cooking. Now, consider whether she's "working" or not, in these scenarios. She's in a restaurant kitchen, working for minimum wage. She's testing a recipe for a new dish on the menu of the restaurant she owns. She's making lunch for and worrying about the future of her unemployed, 36-year-old son who has moved back home. She's preparing a welcoming repast for her husband, who has finally found work up north, and whom she's eager to see during his three-weeks-on, one-week-off rotation. Same picture, different stories. How do you categorize the scenes? Perhaps the first two constitute work, the second two are unpaid work and a labour of love.

Each of us carries our own definition of work in our head. Verbalizing it helps us understand its role in our life. Here's a definition to get your head around, "…work…comprises activities performed within social relations in a sphere of necessity, and work forms are different ways of socially organizing what people have to do to support themselves in a given society."

We also decide the conditions that make work necessary. We're free to determine if work is necessary to provide basic needs of shelter and food or to enjoy the things we think make life worthwhile; are necessary for our mental health; or are necessary for the expression of our essential nature. Most important, each of us alone decides what activity we call work.

What looks like work to one person may not feel like work to another. Out skating one afternoon I run into a friend, now retired, who is teaching fitness classes five times a week to older adults in extended care homes. When I call what she's doing work, she does a double-take. She doesn't call what she's doing work, although she shows up as per a contract and is paid, but she doesn't do it to support herself.

Work Has a New Look

Work is one thing boomers know how to do—most of us have been working for 40 years. Our relationship with work is one of our most durable relationships, and our career defines in large part who we are. But the form work takes has changed dramatically; we've worked differently than our parents, who worked non-stop and retired on cue, at 65.

Our generation is the first to have gone to college and university in large numbers. We flooded the job market in the late sixties and early seventies, employers offering us careers-for-life, generous benefits and a distant reward, a pension. We're the first generation of women to build careers along with marriage, thanks to the resurgence of feminism and the birth control pill. We're the generation that invented career mobility, changing jobs to climb career ladders, and the first generation in which both men and women defined ourselves through work. We're the first generation to enter adulthood with consumer credit—thanks to MasterCard in 1966 and Visa in the 1970s—that helped us spend our unprecedented high earnings—and burden ourselves with debt.

We don't want to do just any work, and few of us will work full-time for an employer. As 2017 begins, only six percent of Canadians over 65 hold full-time jobs, while many others are employed part-time or are self-employed. And, we weigh different issues in this career decision, choosing flexibility as to where, when, and how much we work. The majority of us want part-time, flex-time, casual, or contract work, and take chunks of time off for holidays or to take care of parents or grandchildren, travel, and pursue non-work activities. We want less responsibility, and we are satisfied with less money. As older workers we'll take bigger cuts in earnings than younger workers after being unemployed, because we'll enter less stable work environments and engage in non-standard work, such as part-time and casual work and self-employment. We might move to get work—today's economy is a factor—although we'd rather stay put, near friends, family, neighbours and doctors, unless we move to somewhere warmer or that's close to family. We might even commute long distances to work.

Pressured to do something about our outdated skills, we'll invest time and money in job-related training, upgrading, retraining and a few might even go to university, but education will need to be cost-effective and immediately useful. We need to learn how to search for work in a technological world, and to disprove stereotypes about older workers—that we're technological dinosaurs, in a holding pattern until retirement, unable to get along with younger workers, or have little stamina to do what the job requires.

Role Models Help

If we were familiar with the idea of working in later life, it would be easier, but we have few role models to emulate of people who worked until their 70th birthday or beyond. But wait! We do. Although our parents' generation retired at 65, our grandfathers worked until they were between 65 and 70—if they lived that long. Were they unhappy about working so long? Probably not. We can be inspired and learn from them, as we contemplate working until our 70th birthday or beyond.

These people inspire me.

- Bernie Sanders at 74, Donald Trump at 70, and Hillary Clinton at 69 all stumping in 2016 to serve a four-year term as president of the United States.
- Margaret Atwood, born in 1939, still writing novels and winning prizes.
- Leonard Cohen, who died at 82 in 2016, three weeks after releasing his final album, *You Want It Darker*.
- Alex Ferguson, one of the best-ever football coaches, who retired at 70 in 2013, having led Manchester United to an impressive number of Premier League and European championships.
- Dr. Audrey Griffiths (1922 – 2002), grandmother of my son's childhood friend, who left her Canadian home at 68 to work in Africa as a doctor, a career she had put aside decades earlier to marry and raise children.
- My grandfather who operated his country grocery store until he was 70, and then enjoyed another 10 years of work, inventing devices to use on his prairie farm.

The affinity these men and women had or have for their work reveals a belief about vital wisdom, experience, and know-how, regardless of age. They symbolize a desire to learn and create, and a disregard for negative attitudes about the value and abilities of older people.

What Will Retirement Look Like?

While today's economy is struggling, retirement is undergoing a transformation. Retirement, as a life stage, was implemented for ordinary folk in the late

19th century by Germany's Chancellor Otto van Bismarck, who decreed that 70 (he was then 74) was the age of eligibility for a state pension--though life expectancy was less than 70. Around that time in the U.S., nearly eight out of every ten men (statistics don't discuss women) over 65 were in the workforce, leaving precious few years for retirement.

In the 1960s, the pensionable age dropped to 65 in Canada and most western countries. Around the turn of the millennium, the average retirement age in Canada dropped to 61.2 years, its lowest ever, thanks to two movements. The first was the downsizing purges and early retirement packages doled out to public service workers and corporate employees in the 1990s. The second was the financial industry's Freedom 55 campaign that created an expectation for early retirement at 55, or 60 at the latest.

Around 2012 boomers began making a mass exodus from the labour force through retirement and selective downsizing, creating labour shortages and a drain on company cultures and know-how. Many OECD (Organization for Economic Cooperation and Development) countries (Canada is one of 34 members) began to strategize about how to retain and capitalize on older workers' skills and talents in the late 1990s, although Canada didn't begin developing innovative approaches to keep us on the job until later.

We'll live much longer than previous generations and enjoy better health—living 90 percent of our life in good health and giving us 20 or more years of retirement. It has been predicted that pension systems will go broke as a consequence of the large number of boomers drawing on them. One solution is to delay the drain by changing eligibility and pay-out criteria. Workers may be required to pay into government pension plans for more years to qualify for full benefits (45 years is suggested) and the age of eligibility for pensions and social security could be increased. (Our grandchildren, starting work at 24, likely won't qualify for full benefits until they're 69).

We've thought of retirement as completely stopping work and dedicating ourselves to leisure, the picture of the good life after age 65. However, we may be challenged to enjoy 20 or more years of leisure, not to mention afford them.

All those issues push us further along on our career path.

A Final Word

What combination of work, leisure, and money—three needs we've always balanced—do you want now?

We consider how long we'll work and at what, taking into account our health and our level of energy, the income we'll get in retirement, the state of our personal finances, and the dreams we've held for our later years.

We face an uncharted yet exciting future. In the coming years we'll turn society's picture of work in later years on its head. Those boomers who have already altered their expectations of their sixties and continued to work or embarked on a later-life or encore career can help point the way, and provide hope and inspiration. Forty Canadians boomers generously told me how they were doing it. You'll read their stories in the following chapters. First, let's look at our finances.

Three

Show Me the Money

Seven British oldsters clutch their carry-on bags, anxiously waiting for their flight, bound for The Best Exotic Marigold Hotel, a retirement home in India. Three of them can no longer afford to live in England. Evelyn (played by Judi Dench) is forced to sell her home when she discovers that her recently deceased husband left behind a monstrous debt. Jean (Penelope Wilton) and Douglas (Bill Nighy) have lost the savings they invested in their daughter's start-up internet business.

The 2011 film, *The Best Exotic Marigold Hotel* strikes a chord for many boomers. Much like the film's characters, we've built dreams and expectations about this stage of life—retirement, a future beyond work—based on money we don't have and may never have. Debt and lost savings are only two of the reasons why three of four Canadians of all ages worry their retirement income won't meet their needs. Many boomers don't have enough money to live on now, without working, and some people have never been able to save.

It's time to take a hard look at future income and assets to make financial decisions to carry us into the future. Getting a handle on how much money we need now and in the three stages of ageing that lie ahead can help us determine how much we need to earn, and for how long.

This chapter looks at the income we can expect from pensions, social security programs, and other sources, the debt we're carrying into our "golden years", as well as some ideas about managing the money we have. Activities can help you find out how much to expect from various post-65 income sources. Enter those amounts in the spreadsheet on p. 34 to tally your future income, or use a software spreadsheet.

No Pot of Gold

We've relied on employment to provide most, if not all, of our income prior to age 65. After 65 we can expect income from more sources. Those sources are often grouped and described as three pillars that hold up our financial future. They are:

- the federal, income-tested Old Age Security (OAS) and Guaranteed Income Supplement (GIS) programs,
- the Canada / Quebec Pension Plans (CPP / QPP), and
- private retirement savings in registered pension plans and RRSPs.

I prefer the image of a three-legged stool, each leg representing one of the above sources. In the past the stool has given a stable and comfortable retirement to most Canadians. Today one or more of the legs may be too short or missing altogether.

The First Leg: Old Age Security and the Guaranteed Income Supplement

OAS

The most stable leg on our retirement income stool is Old Age Security (OAS). Most people 65 and over in Canada receive it. It doesn't come automatically at age 65; we have to apply for it.

The maximum monthly OAS cheque was $578.53 in the second quarter of 2017. Amounts are adjusted quarterly, according to the cost of living.

OAS begins to be partially clawed back when net income reaches $73,756, and is increasingly clawed back until it's totally clawed back when net income is $119,615 (based on 2016 income).

OAS makes up a significant percentage of the income of many 65 and older low-income people; it provides almost 30 percent of the income of 65 - 69-year old women and almost 20 percent for men of the same age. OAS replaces roughly 13 percent of the pre-retirement income of average-income earners, according to the Canadian Centre for Policy Alternatives (CCPA).

Residency requirements determine the amount of the monthly cheque.

Activity: OAS

How much will you receive in OAS? Enter the amount in the spreadsheet on p. 34.

GIS

Low-income recipients of the maximum OAS benefit may also receive the Guaranteed Income Supplement (GIS), an income-tested benefit that must be applied for. The amount received is based on marital status and family income.

When a single person's only source of income is OAS, the GIS is $864.09, giving an annual income of $17,544. OAS and GIS together pay less than the after-tax low-income cut-off amount, determined by Statistics Canada (CCPA, 2009). Amounts are adjusted according to the cost of living, but don't keep up with rising wages. People who depend on them slide deeper into poverty over time.

The Second Leg: CPP / QPP
The Canada Pension Plan / Quebec Pension Plan

"I will never collect this," Cora thought, the year CPP contributions were deducted from her first pay cheque as a teacher. The idea that she had to work to have an income was so ingrained that a year of retirement had flown by before she fully accepted that her pension income would continue without her having a job.

Baby boomers were the first generation to pay into the Canada and Quebec Pension Plans (CPP / QPP). Implemented in 1966, CPP and QPP were designed to replace one-quarter of workers' pensionable earnings.

The maximum monthly CPP cheque was $1,114.17 in 2017, but the average is about 60 percent of that or $655.00. You had to pay relatively high premiums on a high income, over a long period of time to get the maximum. On average women receive less than men. In 2009, their cheques were roughly two-thirds of men's, according to the CCPA.

Being out of the workforce for a significant length of time, paying smaller premiums, and beginning to receive CPP before age 65 all reduce your cheque. You can begin to receive CPP as early as age 60, but every month you do reduces the amount by 0.6 percent, or 7.0 percent each year. Receiving CPP at age 60 reduces the amount by 30 percent. Every month you begin to receive CPP after age 65 increases the amount by 0.7 percent, or 8.4 percent a year, and by 42 percent if you begin to receive CPP at age 70.

Two welcome changes: we don't have to quit work to receive benefits, and we don't need a reduced income for two months prior to the start date.

In CPP's early years employees and employers each contributed 1.8 percent of employees' pensionable earnings; that increased to 4.95 percent, today's rate. In 2019 both employee and employer contributions will increase to 5.95 percent to build a reserve for the proposed benefit increase.

In 2016 most provinces tentatively agreed to increase the benefit to one-third of earnings, but boomers will see very little added to their cheques. Millennials (Generation Y, born 1982 to 2002) will be eligible for the full benefit.

Activity: How much CPP will you get?

Contact CPP to find out what you will receive at age 65, and what you'll get if you begin receiving CPP earlier or later than 65. To receive an estimate, type ISP1003 into your browser, print the request form, and complete and mail it to the regional office indicated.

Enter the amount and age you expect to begin receiving CPP into the spreadsheet on p. 34.

You can also enter "view and print your up-to-date Statement of Canada Pension Plan contributions" into your browser, and follow the instructions to see what you've contributed.

CPP and OAS together paid roughly $20,310 a year in 2016, with each at their maximum. That's about $1,600 less than a 40-hour per week minimum-wage job would pay, using an average of all provincial and territorial minimum wages.

Thanks to our social safety net—OAS, GIS—and CPP / QPP, fewer Canadian seniors live in poverty today than they did 50 years ago, when seven out of ten did. (The Conference Board of Canada defines poverty as "the proportion of individuals over age 65 with disposable income less than 50 per cent of the median income of the whole population.") Unfortunately, poverty among the elderly is rising once again, mainly among the increasing number of older women who live alone, because women haven't saved as much for retirement as men have, and are less likely than men to still be working.

The Canadian Centre for Policy Alternatives and the Canadian Labour Congress (an umbrella organization for unions in Canada) propose that CPP should provide half of our pensionable earnings, since workplace pensions are disappearing. Others say that voluntary personal savings programs, which are under-used by many of us and hardly used by low-income earners, should be expanded, to increase retirement incomes.

The Third Leg: Private Retirement Savings

The third leg has two components: Registered pension plans (pension plans) and Registered Retirement Savings Plans (RRSPs).

REGISTERED PENSION PLANS (RPP)

Registered pension plans (RPPs), that are provided by employers or employee groups such as unions, became a cornerstone of retirement income in the twentieth century. In 2013, 37.9 percent of workers in Canada were covered by an RPP, down from 38.5 percent in 2012 and 45 percent in 1992.

Almost half of boomers who started work in 1977 had a pension plan through their work; three-quarters of those were in the public sector while 35 percent were in the private sector. In 2007, 84 percent of public-sector workers had a DB pension, but less than 16 percent of private-sector workers did.

Most unionized workers and public sector employees have been able to rely on **defined-benefit (DB)** pensions. They've been able to predict their pension income according to a formula, agreed upon by the union or employee group and / or the employer, that took into account an employee's age, years of employment and contributions to the plan, and income.

On average a DB pension has paid 67 percent of an employee's salary.

Because DB plans in the private sector are expensive for companies to maintain, many now bar new employees from participating in existing DB plans, are converting their DB plans to defined-contribution plans, or do not offer a pension plan at all.

DB pensions are gradually being replaced by **defined-contribution (DC)** pension plans. Workers who get one can count themselves fortunate. In DC plans it's the contribution that is defined—usually a percentage of an employee's annual salary—not the retirement benefit. The value of an eventual retirement account will be based on the employee's and employer's matching contributions, which are subject to financial markets and a fund manager's or employee's investment savvy, depending on which one manages the investment account.

Skimpy or Empty Pension Pots

We have reasons to worry, says Michael Prince, a professor of social policy at the University of Victoria. Older Canadians will experience a growing vulnerability as more and more companies drop their pension plans, as assets and liabilities of private pension funds disappear, as pension funds are stripped by parent companies or lost in bankruptcies, and as companies disappear.

The amount of money held in private pension plans shrank by about 20 per cent in the global financial crisis that began in 2008, leaving many plans under-funded. It's predicted that many plans will collapse under the weight of longer-living boomers drawing pensions. Drastic measures such as cancelling cost of living allowances, capping monthly cheques at a subsistence level, and requiring new employees to pay higher premiums, may well be implemented to distribute the available money to a growing number of pensioners.

Boomers often withdrew their pension contributions when they left their jobs earlier in their careers, not thinking of retirement. One man said, "It seemed more important to buy a chain saw with my Ontario Pension money than leave it untouched until I retired in 40 years."

Women reach retirement age with pensions 60 percent smaller than men's, on average, or no pension at all. They've often taken lower-paying or part-time jobs that don't offer pension plans, worked fewer years, and contributed for fewer years or never enrolled in an available pension plan. It's not that long ago that women weren't encouraged to sign on to their plan.

Julie's position is not uncommon. She started her nursing career in her late thirties. At 48 she left her marriage with enough money to pay off her line of credit; she relinquished to her husband her half of the farm and all they'd accrued. Before Julie got a full-time position, she patched together part-time jobs so wasn't eligible to participate in the hospital workers' pension plan. At 58, she had eight years into a workplace pension and was making up for lost years by diligently saving in her RRSP and TFSA.

Activity

How much will your receive from your workplace pension when you retire? How much will you receive if you work a few more years? Enter that amount in the spreadsheet on p. 34.

REGISTERED RETIREMENT SAVINGS PLAN (RRSP)

The second piece of private savings is the Registered Retirement Savings Plan (RRSP). Launched in 1957, the RRSP program was designed to provide a retirement savings for workers who had no employer pension. Planners must have expected us to save more than we have.

If the ideal is to retire on 65 to 70 percent of our working income, then we should have set aside 10 to 21 percent of our pre-tax earnings every year for 35 years, says the C.D. Howe Institute. Most of us haven't saved anywhere near that amount. Just 15 to 20 percent of middle-income Canadians who have no benefits in a private pension have saved enough so they don't take a significant drop in retirement income, says a 2016 Broadbent Institute report.

We've had the opportunity to put money into an RRSP since we earned our first paycheque, but most of us were between 35 and 44 before we began to do so, and between the ages of 45 and 54, the peak years for saving, before we got serious about savings in RRSPs. After 55 we cut back our contributions. As well, when the media talked a lot about high consumer debt in 2013, we began to pay down debt instead. Today, the majority of tax filers intend to put money in an RRSP, but only one in four actually does so, a Canadian Imperial bank of Commerce poll found, according to a story on newswire.ca.

Many Canadians earn too little to contribute to an RRSP. Some of us haven't been enticed by the deduction on income that RRSP contributions give us at tax time, nor by the prospect of a healthy retirement income.

Employees in small businesses don't usually receive pensions, but some get an annual contribution to their RRSP from their employer.

Rick was a loyal and dependable employee for 31 years in one company, but was never rewarded with a pension. He did get an annual RRSP contribution, but the amount was always less than the maximum allowed as an income tax deduction. When he left at 59, Rick knew he had to let his RRSP grow until he was 70.

Many of us have raided our RRSPs to tide us over during extended unemployment or to pay off high debt. And, our nest eggs have shrunk in financial disasters—the 27 percent stock market loss in 2008, the 2000 tech bubble burst and other market dives, and unfortunately, even Ponzi schemes

Stephen had done all the right things and was positioned for early retirement until the 2008 crisis cut a swath through his investments. "When I make some money I like to keep it," he said. "You work hard to earn your money, and money doesn't give you happiness, but it certainly sets you up for a lot of freedoms you wouldn't otherwise have. I had put away a fair bit of money that I'd worked hard to get and it was just gone, and it felt panicky." He knew it could happen again. Re-building his retirement account was one of the reasons he went back to work.

Not everyone has income from all three sources—OAS, GIS and CPP—nor would all three provide an adequate income if we did have them. We'll need a fourth leg, another source of income on our income stool.

Add a Fourth Leg: Wealth

In 2016 the C.D. Howe Institute added a fourth pillar to their retirement income model: wealth.

Their wealth pillar includes real estate, financial instruments, businesses, inheritances, insurance, and tax-free savings accounts (TFSAs). Besides their home, it's not clear how many people own secondary property they could derive income from (Chapter 4 talks about our home as a source of income), how many own a business, how many expect an inheritance, and how large might it be. We need more information to answer these questions: Might an inheritance include the parents' home? How is insurance a source of income? We do have data on TFSAs.

Tax-Free Savings Accounts (TFSAs)

Tax-free Savings Accounts (TFSAs) are a new savings program launched in 2009 by the federal government. Their advantage is that the income earned on deposits will never be taxed, although we put after-tax dollars into a TFSA. We can hold bonds, stocks, mutual funds and GICs among other investment products in a TFSA.

The maximum we can have contributed to a TFSA as of 2017 is $52,000. However, only about one in three Canadians had a TFSA in 2013 said a BMO report, and only one in five people who hold a TFSA have maxed out their contribution amount. At any time we can make up the amount not contributed.

A TFSA won't lengthen the leg of the retirement income stool of many Canadians.

Investments

Suze Orman, U.S. financial adviser and money guru, says that income comes in only three ways—through work, as an inheritance or lottery, and as earnings on investments.

In other words, sweat, luck, and savvy. Few people can expect to inherit much money and precious few will win a lottery. Of all possible ways Canadians can invest money, the voluntary savings programs of RRSPs and TFSAs are the primary ones we'll choose, if we have money to invest.

In our sixties, it's late to expect a significant (loosely defined) return on investments, because the older we get the more conservative we become about investing—we have less time to make up for losses.

Many of us aren't sure how to invest. We're confused by the lingo and acronyms of financial products, the conflicting advice given by money advisors, the constant tweaks in savings programs and the introduction of new savings vehicles, and more. Such confusion can prevent a person from even approaching a financial advisor. When we do buy investment products, many of us can't accurately describe their features.

If we can't put more money into retirement savings, we can wait until a later age before we spend the principal, while letting earnings increase the amount in the pot. Meanwhile, we might skim off a portion of the earnings if we need to supplement other income.

Although investing money was not a topic I was initially curious about, several people talked about their investment behaviour.

Stephen resisted spending any of his hard-won investments. "I really am squeamish about drawing from our savings. It's not logical, because we saved for retirement. But now that I'm there, we don't want to touch it! I've also learned that we are not alone in this," *he said.*

Don and Gwen, who had owned an accounting and bookkeeping business, had made retirement investments for years. In retirement, Don checked the status of their investments every morning. Gwen called his morning ritual "his new almost-half-time job".

With a pension that paid monthly bills and earned income that gave Arlene and Carl travel money, Carl felt secure enough to try something different—playing the stock market. Arlene wasn't keen on that so he assured her he would be cautious.

Activity

Do you review your savings or investments regularly?

Will you add money from investments to your monthly income, or, use your savings for an emergency or special purchase?

Enter the amount you'll add each month or year, and the age, in the spreadsheet on p 34.

A Stronger Fourth Leg: Income from Work

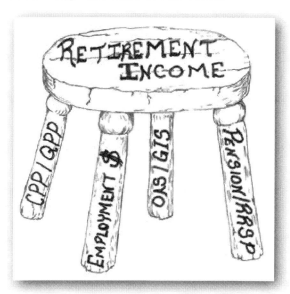

If we'd put away the recommended amount every month for retirement, voluntary savings programs such as RRSPs and TFSAs would set us up nicely for our later years. In theory, they're effective; in practice, not so much. OAS is reliable but too little. The most effective retirement savings option is CPP, a form of forced savings, but many of us don't fare well with it. And, few have the fourth leg, the pillar of wealth.

Canadian boomers will need to screw a stronger fourth leg onto their retirement income stool: earnings from employment. We're in good company. One-fifth of the income of people over 65 in the 34 countries of the Organization of Economic Cooperation and Development comes from earnings from employment and self-employment.

Target after-65 earnings
How much do we need to bring home each month, or year, to have a desirable post-65 income? Enough to just pay the bills? A little more to pay down debt or enjoy extras such as travel? Do we still want to put some money into savings?

Our financial needs change as we age. We're **young-old** at 65 as we enter a 10-year period in which we explore the non-work world, contribute to the community, and spend money on travel and new interests. We're **old** at 75, when we enter a settling-down stage and cut back expenses. At 85, we're **old-old**, when we begin to need money for personal care, just as our disposable income begins to shrink. The old-old stage is so distant and full of unknowns, it's difficult to predict how much we'll need, especially if we'll need to include the cost of personal care.

These stages and features don't describe everyone's life, but that shouldn't stop us from calculating a ballpark figure of what our income will be after age 65.

You've entered the amount and age you expect to begin receiving each income source into a spread sheet. Now you can estimate how much money you want to earn from work and for how many years.

Consider this: do you still want to have money in the bank when you die so you can leave a nestegg for your kids or charitable organization? Would you like to die with a zero balance? Or are you okay with leaving debt behind? It's a matter of personal choice.

Rhiannon retired at 60 from a demanding career in the food science industry. At 61 she began studying to earn a certificate as a career practitioner. Two years later, although she had a good pension, Rhiannon was enjoying her new half-time job, helping people with brain injuries return to work. After a year she planned to start a consulting business. Her target was to earn $700 to $1000 a month until she was 70, to supplement her pension, CPP and OAS. She wouldn't touch her savings until she was 70.

Ruth, at 65, worked two days a week for about 30 percent more than minimum wage—and loved getting paid for every 15 minutes of overtime. Because she had a healthy pension from teaching, nearly half her earnings were taxed. The rest topped up holidays.

Jim's income came from working part-time at a casino and his business, selling collectibles in an antique mall and on eBay. Self-employment gave him half of what he needed each month.

"I need a salary," said Norm, whose earnings had depended on commissions for much of his life. "That's what I finally realized. If I work for an hour, I have to be paid for an hour. And I need that bit of structure. One reason I work is have money to do the things I want to do. Not extravagant things, just getting out and doing things such as skiing with my granddaughters."

Employment Insurance
Employment Insurance (EI) won't be a reliable short-term measure if we work part-time or in short contracts. As well, if we qualify for EI, we may run out of benefits before we land the next job; and if we turn to self-employment, we won't be eligible for EI.

Retiring in the Red

We didn't expect to reach 65 and still owe money. A 2010 Royal Bank survey found that four of 10 Canadians carry debt into retirement. An Equifax (a credit reporting agency) report in 2016 said that Canadians over 65 owe $15,238 in consumer debt, a number that doesn't include mortgages. We're carrying debt on credit cards, lines of credit, car loans, and high-interest instalment loans.

Debt isn't necessarily a problem, depending on the kind of debt it is, how much it costs to carry it, when it grows faster than our income, and our ability to pay it off. But when we dread opening our bills, when we can't see when we'll ever pay it off, when we're paying a lot in interest and have no money for the finer things, when it pushes us to work when working itself creates problems, then debt is a problem.

Mortgage debt
Some of us hold first and second mortgages. When housing prices were rising rapidly, many people used their equity to finance renovations or buy more expensive houses, gambling that equity would continue to increase. When the housing bubble fizzled, our debt increased relative to assets. In most regions of Canada we can't expect to float out of this debt situation on another housing bubble. We'll look more closely at mortgages and property losses in the next chapter, The Roof over Our Heads.

Those who entered the housing market late, after divorce, may still have a mortgage. They either bought a home for themselves or took out a second mortgage to buy out their spouses' share of the property.

When Gene and his wife separated, he kept the house and took out a second mortgage to buy out her half and to pay off their consumer debt. He planned to retire at 70, when his first mortgage would be paid, but he expected to never pay off his second mortgage, leaving him short of money to do some of the things he'd always hoped to do in retirement.

Mary and her husband were on a mission to save the old general store in the nearby village. They found a partner to restore the heritage building—turning it into a rentable living space and boutique space—and mortgaged their house to finance the project. Part way into renovations the deal fell apart. About the same time, Mary was diagnosed with breast cancer and couldn't land work contracts. They sold the building and lived on the proceeds while she underwent treatment. Eventually she was back at work securing contracts, but they were left with a mortgage.

CONSUMER DEBT

We may whittle away on our mortgages after we retire, but we increase our credit card debt. Between 2003 and 2005 the median debt of Canadians over 70 was $15,610, which suggests we don't adjust our spending habits in post-earning years. Of the 70,000,000 credit cards in use in Canada—about two for each Canadian—the monthly balance is paid off on only 64 percent. Interest rates, about 19.5% on premium or rewards cards, can strand us on the debt treadmill, while we pay a huge amount in interest.

Activity

You charge a cruise costing $4200 on your rewards credit card. If you make only minimum monthly payments, about how long will it take to fully pay for your cruise? *The answer is on page 33.*

- A. 5 years, 4 months
- B. 27 years, 8 months
- C. 52 years, 1 month

RETIRE CONSUMER DEBT

We have three ways to get rid of debt: earn more and/or reduce expenses; convert or refinance it; and legally divest ourselves of it. How do people cut expenses? Is converting debt an option? What legal means are available?

LIVE ON LESS

> *Pierre had learned...that man is created for happiness, that happiness is within him, in the satisfying of natural human needs, and that all unhappiness comes not from lack, but from superfluity.*
>
> – WAR AND PEACE, LEO TOLSTOY

If predictions are accurate, that we'll have to live on as little as 50 percent of our income from work and take a five percent cut in our standard of living in retirement, it follows that we'll have to adjust our spending. But, how easy is it to live on less?

If we no longer work, some spending cuts will come in transportation and clothing, and we won't need to buy as many services and products to support an employment lifestyle. We'll feel some relief when our mortgage and consumer debts are paid off, and we'll be able to take advantage of seniors' discounts for movies, concerts, public transportation, banking, recreation and adult education classes, and more.

For the first time ever, at 69, Josée calculated her post-retirement income, when she quit work in two years. She wasn't looking forward to changing her spending habits since she'd always bought pretty well what she wanted. High on her list of things that make life worthwhile was going to The Bahamas twice a year—going once would feel like a sad compromise. However, since she didn't know how much she'd get in various pensions, it was too soon to say if she'd have to give up the second trip. She wondered if her husband would be willing to help her a bit with holidays, though asking him would be a stretch: her streak of independence stopped her from relying on others. She thought she could possibly follow a budget and was considering what things she and her husband would forgo on their retirement income. But

Josée didn't want to change her lifestyle, so she began to read books about financial management and was developing an interest in the stock market.

Carl and Arlene were surprised to discover that they didn't need as much money to live on as they had thought prior to his retirement, but the question of when to dip into savings was perplexing. Like Stephen, they were afraid to dip in too soon.

Karen and Ole joked that the simple lifestyle they'd adopted on BC's remote central coast was good training for living on a pension when they finally semi-retired, and when Ole would work only part-time.

Graham worked on an as-needed basis at a hospital, commuting by bus when called in to work. He had sold his car and rented one when he needed to. Otherwise he walked or used a bicycle and public transit to get groceries and to get around town.

For PJ it was a matter of choice. She had no desire to travel, but said, "Life is too short to have cheap shoes or bad coffee. My mother would roll over in her grave at the thought of me paying $17 a pound for coffee, but I like good coffee. I'm not particularly worried about money, but I'd like to make sure I don't have to enter a housing situation I'm not comfortable with."

Living on a low income can restrict our social life; that can affect our health. It may be too costly to meet friends for coffee or lunch, and perhaps we drive the car only when necessary. We need to find ways to stay engaged that don't break the budget.

CONVERT DEBT

Over 12 years, Bette and Earl racked up unmanageable debt on several credit cards. The bank made them cut up their cards in order to borrow against their house in a home equity line of credit (HELOC). At a much lower interest rate, they began to slowly pay off the line of credit, although it was a struggle to meet their target some months. Since his retirement at 58, they'd lived on his pension. Bette's health prevented her from working, but Earl had started to make a bit of extra money selling the flies he tied to local fishing and country stores. Owing on the HELOC would limit the amount they could borrow if they ever needed money for more urgent needs, and if interest rates increased, they would feel the pinch.

They found it hard to scale down their spending habits, but were determined to live without credit cards, fearing the worst case scenario of losing their home if they went into debt again.

When the usual options aren't enough

Ten percent of those who declared bankruptcy in 2014 were 65 or older, and the number of Canadians over 55 who declare bankruptcy is increasing.

In 2016 Canadians owed $1.67 for every $1.00 of income, an amount of indebtedness that's unmanageable when income drops. Debt often follows job loss, business failure, and medical problems and illness that leave you unable to work. It also follows when a child fails on a mortgage or business loan a parent has co-signed. It's not unusual to be hit by two or more problems at once.

The Bankruptcy and Insolvency Act offers three ways to deal with unmanageable debt. The Orderly Payment of Debts program (OPD), available in Alberta, Saskatchewan, Nova Scotia and Prince Edward Island, allows you to consolidate and repay all non-secured debt at a low interest rate under the protection of a court order, usually within four years. The other two ways, consumer proposals and bankruptcy, are available across Canada.

Marilyn, at 58, moved into an apartment after her marriage failed with half of the household belongings she and her husband had accumulated. She bought everything she didn't already have on credit: furniture on a buy-now-pay-later plan, and linens and clothes for work on two department store credit cards (interest rates of more than 28 percent). Then, for five years Marilyn paid little more than the minimum required on her debt, making little headway reducing the amount she owed. She couldn't get a consolidation loan; the debt was too high, her income too low and she had no assets. A debt management course helped her see that the interest she had paid on the debt had more than paid for the things she'd bought, and pinching pennies for years to come wasn't likely to get rid of the debt. Marilyn declared bankruptcy and then began to save what she could for retirement, far down the road.

With all three options provincial credit regulations determine how much of your income and assets you can keep and how much must go to repay creditors.

Helping the Kids

We may want to leave things better for our kids, and our generation has been in a position to help them get a good start in education, housing and business. If we give them money, how much should we give and for what? Our help can create problems if we help them to the extent that they don't learn to rely on themselves to make their own way, or help them so that it cripples our financial future, or both.

Money given to kids is best designated up front as a gift, as part of their future inheritance, or as a loan with conditions about repayment. There should be no grey area about repayment because that can lead to resentment later. We may give cash or co-sign a loan, and some of us may even use our home as collateral to make the down payment on our kids' houses. However, using home equity to finance children's or grandchildren's education isn't recommended, since there are less expensive alternatives for borrowing for education.

A gift or loan to children should meet three conditions: we must be able to afford to give it, our child must need it, and we must be the best or only possible lender. If the money is a loan, we need to be in a position to lose it. If we co-sign a child's loan, we'll have to repay it if our child can't.

Some people find a solution in giving small and specific financial help, such as buying grandchildren's school supplies each fall, or buying a second car. Giving instrumental help is an alternative to giving money, such as looking after grandchildren to reduce our children's child care costs or helping out in their business to reduce overhead. In chapter 5 The Roof over Our Heads, you'll read how some boomers support their adult kids when they move back home.

Our kids may take care of us when we're old. We can give them a more secure financial future by staying productive.

A Last Word

Boomers are a lost generation regarding pension reform, says the Canadian Centre for Policy Alternatives. Our political leaders have lacked foresight and political will. Any of governments' current efforts to resolve the crisis won't help us. Boomers are often maligned for spendthrift tendencies and failing to plan for the future. Perhaps the abundance we grew up with and an "I'll think about it tomorrow" mindset blinded us to a problem that has been brewing for decades. Regardless, we're in a tight position. Predictions say we're going to run out of money, and aging boomers will break the CPP and health care banks.

As a society we have paid little attention to one solution. It's not to head off to a Best Exotic Marigold Hotel in a distant country, although a few will do that. Rather, it's to attach that fourth leg—earnings from employment—to our retirement income stool. Our challenge is to find work that generates the desired income and is satisfying.

Answer: The answer to the question on p. 28 is C: 52 years and one month.

Activity

Map your post-65 income: This chart can help you decide when to add a new income source, such as income from work or sale of your home. If you prefer, use an online retirement nestegg planner or see a retirement planning adviser. Project your income for as many years as you can provide reasonably accurate amounts.

INCOME SOURCES	201___ Age___	201___ Age___	201___ Age___	...
CPP				
OAS				
GIS				
RRSP/RIF				
TFSA				
Work income				
Pension				
LIF				
Annuity				
Home equity				
Inheritance				
Rental income				
Other				
Total				

Four

Sixty Is the New...Sixty

*There's a catchy new saying going around:
"Sixty is the new forty."*

I woke up the morning of my 65th birthday—and laughed out loud. Here I was, at that dreaded landmark age, the day I'd be old. But the morning was no different than most others—it promised to be a sunny, warm September day, and I was standing on the doorstep of discount heaven. At dirt cheap prices I could buy a seniors' annual bus pass, a year's membership to the art gallery, a ticket to a movie, and eat supper at a senior-friendly restaurant. I did none of those, but the tingle I felt reminded me of Christmas morning when I was a child, excited to open presents. The discounts weren't especially grand, but they were welcome. And in a month, OAS cheques would begin to drop into my bank account.

    I was in the midst of making decisions that would affect my life on a grander scale, decisions that required some tough thinking. For the most part I've had a life of good fortune. I've been tripped up a time or two and committed various acts of folly, but I've developed a bit of wisdom and character—or at least I hope so. Sixty-five years of life experience were influencing the decisions I faced:

- Should I sell my house and move? If so, to where?
- What kind of work should I do?
- Where would I like to travel?
- How should I spend my money?
- And the big question, how should I spend my remaining years?

I'm not alone. We boomers face an explosion of decisions in our sixties, forcing us to reflect on our lives. I assessed what I'd done with my time and accomplished with my efforts, pondered how many more years I'd have, and wondered—somewhat fearfully—how many of those would be good.

"Sixty is the new 40", we hear, comparing our generation at 60 years to 40-year-olds of previous generations. That morning, I didn't feel 40 or any age in particular, but the calendar said I was getting on in years, creating a yawning mismatch between my age and my sense of self.

Our Upbringing Affects How We Work

The historical period we grew up in affects who we've become. The sixties molded us—front-end boomers born between 1946 and 1954—in a way that makes us different from the Silent Generation that preceded us (those born prior to 1945 who were to be seen but not heard) and the latter half of the baby boom, born between 1954 and 1964, the GenJonesers. We grew up in unprecedented affluence and peace, which has influenced our penchant to buy. Our parents, having read Dr. Spock's revolutionary ideas in *The Common Sense Book of Baby and Child Care* (1946), were affectionate and attentive to our needs. We hid under our desks in nuclear bomb drills, and went to school in shifts to accommodate the burgeoning number of kids.

Existential philosophy and humanistic psychology gave birth to the human potential movement in the 1960s and '70s, which flowered into personal growth and relationship enhancement workshops and self-help groups. The concept of self-actualization, introduced by Abraham Maslow in the hierarchy of needs, led to an interest in one's self. Self-improvement wormed itself into every aspect of life, including work.

We tore the brown wrapper off things sexual, consuming *Our Bodies Ourselves* and *The Joy of Sex*. If women didn't read *The Feminine Mystique* and *The Female Eunuch*, then feminist ideas filtered through on the pages of *Chatelaine* magazine. We were the first generation to use readily available, effective birth control, deciding when and how many children we'd have. That allowed women to focus on careers. Women shed girdles and hiked up hemlines, while men grew Beatles' hair and sported moustaches and bell-bottoms, all symbols of the new generation.

We took to the road, often on our thumbs. With *Europe on $5 a Day* (1957), reborn as *Europe on $10 a Day* in 1972, we traveled, interrupting further education or before taking a first job.

In the 1960s and early '70s, the women's liberation movement, a revival of the feminist suffrage movement of the early 1900s, focused attention on equality for women in the workplace. Still, many women expected to get married in their early twenties, work a year or two before quitting to have children and returning to work when the kids were older.

In the late sixties, when a job interviewer asked me what I wanted to be doing in two years' time, I guilelessly said that I wanted to be married and live in Calgary. The interviewer may have given me one point for honesty, but she didn't hire me. Women planning long-term careers was a distant idea. It was hard to break the glass ceiling and hard to go back to work after maternity leave. Their job was to take care of the home; men were to bring home the paycheck. Women who worked were told they were taking a job away from a man—a sentiment that lingered from the years after the Second World War, when women filed out of factories to make way for returning soldiers.

Women stood on a great divide as they sought equality in earnings and family leadership, bringing change for men and the family. *One women, Jan, found that principles of equality brought confusion. "Women understood that we needed to support ourselves, even if we were with someone who made a good living. But I screwed myself when I was married. My husband always made more money than I did, yet I insisted on paying half. That was foolish," she said.*

If marriages weren't forever, then Canada's new Divorce Act (1968, revised in 1986) could remedy the situation, ushering in an era of more working women.

Couples became happier when the kids left home, when they were finally past the heavy lifting of establishing homes and families. Kids mostly launched, we began to save for retirement while taking care of parents—taxiing them to doctors, helping them move to their final home, planning memorial services and settling their estate. Today, some kids have come back home to live, putting us in the middle of a jammed sandwich, often babysitting grandchildren. *Bunny said, "Some days I would just like to say to hell with it all. I don't want to be the sandwich generation, but that's where I'm at right now, so I deal with it as best as I can."*

'They' say we're responsible for a myriad of social problems, including those of our children. We're criticized for being idealists, yet wasteful and self-centred. We've been resented since we took all the jobs in the 1960s and 1970s, leaving none for boomers born in the decade after us. Today, boomers still at work are blamed for the difficulties youth face finding work. Fear grows with predictions of the collapse of Canada's healthcare system, if not the whole economy, under our aging weight. This gray wave, this demographic tsunami that we are, presents problems for politicians and social planners, and for ourselves.

Now "old", we have a role in creating solutions to meet our own needs.

Is Sixty Young or Old?

How we answer that question may influence our decisions about work.

We are physically, psychologically and behaviourally younger than our grandparents at the same age, although it probably wasn't fashionable in their day to think of oneself as young. Apparently we think of ourselves as seven years younger than we actually are. *Gene summed it up: "I don't think of myself as old except when I get my birthday. Or I look in the mirror or see myself in a recent picture, and I do look old. But I'm not going to try to be young and whipper-snapper."*

Thinking that we're old makes us more likely to be so, since 'oldness' is more a social construction than a biological fact. We age physically, but more importantly, we age in our minds, in our attitudes, stereotypes, prejudices, assessments of what we're able to do, and changes in behaviour.

Ageist prejudices were hard-wired into society's consciousness in the 1920s when research said our abilities begin to deteriorate around age 40. Recent research shows exactly what about us deteriorates and why—it's not so bad—and what about us is stronger.

Meanwhile, ageist labels such as "the ageing", "near senior" and "senior", and put-downs such as "geezer" can make us feel old and even marginalize us. Such labels don't fit our concept of self. *I asked people if they thought of themselves as a senior citizen. "Gosh, no" Linda said at 64, laughing.*

Older people in TV sitcoms don't seem to work, are caricatures of the aged, and eccentric and foolish, yet we're to vaunt our wisdom and think of ourselves as elders. In fantasy movies, older characters have magical qualities—think Alec Guinness in *Star Wars*. However, producers and directors themselves are putting on years, so their ideas of what makes good film may be changing.

Forty-odd years ago the French termed the 25 years between 50 and 75 The Third Age, a more neutral concept, and slipped it neatly into the life trajectory between middle age and old, pushing back old age. *Zoomer* magazine portrays older Canadians as upbeat and active.

Boomers are the third largest consumer sector and the target of the "silver economy," a new term that describes the purchasing power and ways in which an aging population is an economic opportunity. There is significant job growth in new products and services. You've seen the ads: financial products such as reverse mortgages; good-driver, reduced-rate car insurance; mobility-maintaining devices; health and wellness products and services to maintain independence; clothing and fashion; health tourism and exotic cruises.

Stereotypes about Age and Work

A large part of our identity comes from what we do, our work. Most of us have worked our entire adult life. Besides giving us a position in society, a sense of accomplishment, and a place where we feel valued, we develop a worker identity. But does a worker identity have a best-before date?

David grew up believing that work was central to his life, tha*t "You are your work. That's how men were brought up. So much of our generation's identity* is what you do, so it's hardly surprising that people want to keep doing it," he said. To David and others, the usual follow-up to the work identity is the retired identity. "We grew up with that, too. When I started with the railway, it was 'I'm going to get a pension in 30 years and life is wonderful.' Everybody in that office, to a man, would have said, 'This is a retirement job.'"

The worker identity reaches an expiration date: beyond our mid-sixties we shouldn't be working. That may be why we see so many prejudices about older workers in the workplace. Such opinions can be spoken aloud or implied, and can feel painful when applied to us.

While Rhiannon was studying to become a career practitioner, she would listen to classmates complain about encountering 60-year old clients who were looking for work. In her sixties, Rhiannon shuddered at the dismissal in their voices. Later, when she encountered clients also in their 60s who applied stereotypes to themselves, she would ask them what about their age made them feel there were restrictions. "It may be fear or that people think they're too old, but I wait for them to tell me. It's a mindset. I never think I'm too old."

Josée, 69 and a supervisor in a health agency, refused to tell people her age. She recalled a management meeting in which the conversation, spoken in a nasty tone, turned to 'a woman in her seventies working in a government job.' Josée had kept mum, aware that the stereotype could easily be applied to her.

Do we say something about out-and-out prejudice in our social world? Josée listened to the chat at a cousin's fiftieth birthday party: "Everyone was moaning and groaning about turning 50," she said. "I was wondering, do I say anything or not. I kept quiet, and they were quiet about me, too. Their mindset must be 'My god, she's 60!'"

Opposition to older workers in the labour force can be intense. I was floored by a BBC news story in which a teacher on a British civil service picket line shrieked to the camera, "Do people really want 68-year-olds teaching their children?" She and others were on strike against the government's proposed increase in age to qualify for pensions. She didn't say what it was about a 68-year old teacher that wasn't acceptable, but I hope when she approaches the new pensionable age of 68, she values her contributions to children's education.

Gene, 67, one of the oldest counsellors in his department, wouldn't let age be a barrier as he worked with a wide-age range of staff and clients. Among his colleagues was one he considered a buddy. "He's in his 30s and teases me about being an old geezer, 'Are you going to remember that, Gene?' It's part of the fun we have." Gene didn't find such teasing about his age a problem. He knew that his colleagues appreciated him and his experience, and often turned to him for advice.

Doug said, "We were almost conditioned to think if you didn't retire by 55, you know, Freedom 55, and make room for young people coming up, you're a bad person. Now, it's the opposite: 'We don't want you to get out of the workforce.' I think as more and more people realize, especially if they keep their bodies in reasonably good shape, that working past 65 is not such a bad thing. It keeps you mentally sharp and hopefully, it will do something for you physically as well." Yet regarding his political career, Doug said, "I knew it was my last shot at getting elected at territorial government, because I'm getting too bloody old. Not in my mind, and physically I think I'm okay, my mind and memory seem to be okay, too. But I think to people at 67, you're getting along, and maybe it's time to realize your limitations. It's how we're seen." As a minister in the Yukon government, Doug was able to look for competent, retired seniors to put on boards and committees.

So strong are social stereotypes of older people that it's not uncommon for us to under-value ourselves. But employers are looking to hire people with experience.

Bunny was sure that no employer would hire a former government employee in her early fifties. When thoughts of returning to work began to niggle, her financial adviser suggested she work in his business. She responded, "They won't hire me. I'm old. They want somebody young and attractive." You never know, he had countered. At the job interview, Bunny was asked the typical questions about what she had to offer and what she could bring to the company. She answered that she brought years of experience working with numbers and balancing things, and then quipped, "I guess you can tell by the colour of my hair I won't be going on maternity leave any time soon." A few weeks later she was offered part-time work. Four years later Bunny realized her worth in dollars, with experience in government payroll and pensions and as a supervisor. At 58 she decided, "I have a few good years left in me. I can work full-time, and the government can get a good 10 years out of me," she said after two years back at the government.

Ruth, 65, a former teacher and retired five years when we met, got hired and even approached for jobs because she was seen as age-responsible. She had no wish to continue her professional career; she preferred part-time service work where she could meet people and give structure to her time.

We may struggle with our own ageing, with the notion that we have a best-before date. We'll run into ageist stereotypes at work, get the feeling we're not valued and have nothing to contribute. We may challenge it; barely tolerate it, let it slide off our backs, or not notice it. We need to value ourselves, know what we have to contribute, find a place for ourselves, and get on with the job.

Knowing Ourselves

> *If you don't know yourself by the time you're 60, then you really should be thinking about it.*
>
> — JAN

In *Leap! What Will We do with the Rest of Our Lives?* Sara Davidson says that in this period she labels "the narrows"—a rough passage to life's next stage—we are called to reflect on our lives.

We ask whether we accomplished something that will benefit others. Did we create something that will outlast us? If we feel satisfied with what we've done, we develop a sense of fulfilment and acquire wisdom, but it can be disconcerting if we see our life as mismanaged, with botched decisions and wacky priorities. Burdening ourselves with regret and guilt, and not forgiving ourselves or others can mess up the future.

Norm echoed this attitude. He admitted to having not known himself well at certain times in his life. He had expected to do good work for people and make lots of money in the life insurance industry, but he summed up that career effort as "a huge unmitigated disaster." With reflection he had accepted the "mistakes." Seeing *the need to work until he's 69 or 70 to make up for the "profligacy" of his youth, Norm said it's sad if people don't learn life's lessons, learn about their own preferences, and feel that they can't move away from situations that aren't working for them. "I've got more growing to do. I don't know what's out there for me or what's on my path, but I want to go down that path. What I strive for is to grow as a man, as a person. Work helps that."*

Resentment toward the school board that failed to acknowledge her concerns, never mind resolve them, had eaten at Ruth after she retired. Realizing that carrying it around in her head could turn her into "a bitter old lady", she decided to leave it in the past to build a more likeable, positive life.

Few of us haven't been kicked around at least a bit by life. Divorce is one of those kicks. *"Me doing things for me probably was a big downfall to my marriage," Jim said at 60. "In my mind I was doing things that were contributing to my marriage, but in reality, I was doing things for me. That weighs on me."* He felt "gutted" by the end of his marriage; friends helped him regain emotional strength. And although he never thought of himself as a happy person, he was becoming content with his "less than perfect" life. Julie, at 58, regretted staying too long with her abusive husband, but with little support at the time, she chalked it up to having done the best she could.

Bunny fell into a dark tail-spin after taking her husband off life-support. Grieving, she quit work and soon began to feel she was nearing the end of her productivity. A few years of part-time work helped rebuild her sense of worth. "I have lived life. Life kicked me in the ass, so I've gained that life experience, too," she said with determined pride.

Our Changing Body

We leak when we sneeze. We get the flu shot, have our bone density analyzed, and undergo prostate screenings. We put on weight and have a tough time losing it. We're less active and may damage something if we plunge into a fitness regime. Now that we have time to travel, health insurance rates climb.

Our health and energy level affect how long and how we'll work. Many of us struggle to push ourselves over an extended period.

At 67, Gene would come home more tired at the end of the day than he used to, with little energy to go out in the evening. Jim chose to work part-time, since full-time was four days of 12-hour shifts followed by three days off. At 61, he could force himself to do full-time, but he'd be done-in at the end of the seven-day cycle. Susan, 61, maintained a black belt in karate, but she couldn't gather up the energy required to work at an intense pace writing policy she didn't morally support. Jan was starting to find the stress of contract deadlines draining, although she still enjoyed the adrenalin they gave her. Karen saw that 25 years of running a trucking business were taking a toll on her husband Ole's health. If he kept it up, a crisis could do him in, so they sold the business.

Julie said, "Work takes more energy than before. I'm working full-time. When I come home after a long day, I don't have enough energy, at 59, to be involved in many activities. I'll probably work full-time 'til I'm 65. I can see myself working beyond that, depending on my health and level of energy. I could continue full-time or do part-time or locum." And, she no longer had the energy to do a master's degree, which would have opened the door to teaching nursing students. With hindsight, she realized she should have continued studying after the nurse practitioner (NP) program.

Lynne, embarking on a teaching career at 56, didn't have the abundant energy as she'd once had, something her new work might require.

Gerard, at 59, was looking for work for the third time in his 25-year career as a project manager in construction companies. He'd had two long periods of unemployment in his career when he'd been let go after one merger and during a recession. In his twenties and thirties he would burn the candle at both ends; now, employers expected out of him what they expected of the 25-year old in the next office, but Gerard said, "I like to say I work smarter, not harder. When someone hires me, they get my knowledge, my experience. I'm not going to make as many mistakes as the young person, but I'm not going to put in 12-hour days."

Health events can change our life and spark a sense of urgency. *Divorce and two knee replacements, which left her barely able to walk for a while, made Jan think hard about who she was.* "I'm keenly aware of the need to do things while you're still able and to enjoy yourself after sixty," she said. "I realized that it was all bound up for me. I really like my work, and would like to keep on to some degree, probably for the rest of my life." *Gene's one knee replacement—the other knee would need it soon—made him less steady than he used to be. It didn't affect his ability to work, but now he was afraid to climb a ladder to get on the roof, and he had quit downhill skiing.*

It's a fast lane out there, faster than the one we entered decades ago. Few of us want to step into the flow. On the brighter side: we don't get as sick as often as young people do, and that makes us more desirable as workers.

Sixty...A Wake-up Call

At 65, I said to a friend, "If I live to my life expectancy age, I've got 17 or 18 more years left," then felt stunned by the realization. How did I want to use those remaining years? How many would be in good health? Would physical capabilities permit me to do the things I still wanted to do?

Our sixties give a clarion call. Many of the people I talked to told me about what being 60 had given them: a live-now attitude, a need to plan the future, a bargaining to extend years, and a new confidence.

LIVE LIFE NOW

"The dress rehearsal is over. We go through life getting ready to do whatever. All of a sudden it's upon us. We can no longer put off things. We have to do them. We don't know how much longer we have left to do them in. My whole life has been a bucket list," Jim said, having cottoned on to the notion long before the film of that name made it popular.

Susan believed that we know how many days we're going to have. She intended to enjoy each day and to spend money. William said, "I think in life, from one day to the next, we're just rolling the dice once we get beyond 60. Some of my very good friends have passed away. I vowed I would try to make the most of every instant."

To PJ, time moved rapidly. "Young people think that it's the end of the world when they turn 25. Thirty isn't the end of the world. Forty isn't the end of the world, nor is 50 or 60. By the time you realize that, the days are going faster and faster," she said.

MAKE PLANS

We can't control the future, but creating a picture of what we want gives purpose to each day. Some spoke of their plans to spend the coming years.

Rhiannon had always made 10-year plans, but recently had decided that five-year plans made more sense, although it scared her to think in such a short block of time. The last 10 years had been an intense transition period—exiting her life-long career as a manager in the food industry, earning a certificate in adult and continuing education and a diploma as a career practitioner, and beginning work in the field. She would slow down by working part-time or casually in the coming years, sell her condos, find ways to share life with her partner who lived a thousand kilometres away, move to the coast and buy a cabin, and travel for six months every other year.

Doug was thinking about his future in politics. "If I get out of this when I'm 67 or 68, what I will probably do before I leave is make sure that I have a couple of boards of commissions or something like that that I can go on. Either that, or as I've often said, I'll probably get out of territorial politics in the spring and municipal elections will be coming up in the fall, so I'll be okay."

When Jim made definite plans, such as how long he'd work for an employer, things didn't always work out, so he preferred to live day-to-day. He'd lost a long-term job when one company folded. Later, the loss of his marriage and home had devastated his world.

BE CONFIDENT

"You've got the confidence that comes with life experience." Elle said. "It doesn't matter what your experiences are, you've made it to this point. That gives you a confidence that comes only with living X number of years. You feel good about where you're at. And, if you don't, you do something about it."

Jim had that confidence. "Turning 60 changed a whole bunch of things. It gave me more of that 'I-don't-really-care' attitude. What can somebody do to me that is going to bother me that much? Do I care about losing a good job? No, because I'll find something else. I'm that kind of person."

Josée could look at her varied career with forgiveness and appreciated the background and skills she had developed. She had recently cleaned out her hoard of books and materials gathered at years of conferences, no longer needing to hold onto it all to prove she knew something. "It's bizarre," she said, "not having confidence within myself."

BARGAIN FOR MORE YEARS

Thinking about the future can lead to thinking about our mortality, and bargaining to stretch the good years. Gene said, "All my grandparents died when *they were very old. I have a picture of myself living about as long as my dad, so I've still got twenty-some years. But I might outlive that, since I don't smoke."*

To Stephen, purpose is key to living a long life happily, but, "Without health the outcome is obvious. More boomers are eating properly and working out than ever before—including me!"

Be Inspired by Role Models

*We are all plain people.
Without heroes we don't know how far we can go.*

BERNARD MALABEAU

When haven't you said, "If he / she can do that, so can I." Role models inspire and motivate us when we're young and in every stage of life, even now. They can shine a light on the path as we negotiate this new phase and give us an image of what life might look like when we've finally arrived.

I asked everyone if someone who worked in their later years had influenced their decision to have a working future.

Parents, if they're mentally active and engaged in personally rewarding interests, can still inspire. *When Jan cast her gaze into the future, she saw herself working as a writer, at least part-time into her 80s, in part modelling herself after her father, who still wrote every day in his 90s.*

Don admired Tony La Russa, the former manager of the St. Louis Cardinals, who retired in 2012 at 67, going on to do some work for the Commissioner of Baseball before becoming an analyst and adviser to the Arizona Diamondbacks. La Russa also released One Last Strike: Fifty Years in Baseball, Ten and a Half Games Back, and One Final Championship Season, *co-written with sports writer Rick Hummel, proof, perhaps, that writing that one book, one's life story, waits inside everyone, and is a natural career extension.*

Stephen was intrigued by one of the owners of the food processing company where he worked. The 82-year old, who Stephen thought might have been a hard-nosed businessman in his heyday, was a cheerleader, hustling around the plant each day, talking to all his people. He "checks in on the books and pushes the guys he thinks are getting lazy," said Stephen. "He's out there, participating, contributing, trying to make a difference."

Josée appreciated her mother, who had expanded the business of the art gallery she and her husband had owned. Josée's mother had worked to her mid-seventies, employing her social skills effectively in business relationships.

Another's failure to pursue their dream may spur you on. Mary's passion for writing may have come from her mother, but Mary was a mother herself before she set out to find out about her mother, a talented woman who had written poetry, short stories and several scripts for television. "She could have done 'it' but she didn't have the courage. That's where she influenced me – how her life unfolded and for the fact that she never pursued that dream. I thought, it's time that I did. I have a dream and I'm going to follow it. Amen."

A Final Word

Sixty is not the new 40. Sixty is 60, the beginning of a decade we're each challenged to live according to our needs.

This decade can echo with satisfaction, contentment and even excitement.

Our parents might have aged gracefully, but we'll age actively—the key to wellbeing. One course of action can help to fund our increased longevity and help us to age actively—work.

Activity

Adopt a role model: You can use the term role model, mentor or simply a person you admire. Think of someone who is your age or older who inspires you about how to live this next stage of your life. He or she may be someone you personally know or be a public figure. What does he or she do that you admire? Which character traits do you admire? What personal qualities do they use to live their life? Often a quality we like in someone else is one of our own, just waiting to be developed. Try to understand the beliefs that drive how they make decisions and live their life. Can you imitate those qualities?

His or her behaviour may challenge a belief you have about yourself. Ask yourself, "Why isn't he or she too old to do that?" Chances are he or she doesn't accept being too old as a reason not to do something, whether it's starting a business, going to university, learning to sail or play a musical instrument, or going back to work.

We can learn by observing others' behaviour. If they can do "it", why can't you?

Sandra Konrad

Activity

Check your stereotypes about age 60

Ageist stereotypes surround us. We get accustomed to beliefs that say how older people should look and behave, and how society values—or under-values—older people. We may not realize when we or others say those beliefs, nor counter them with more realistic thoughts.

Ageist stereotypes can be as small as "I'm having a senior's moment" to put-downs like "Nobody wants to hire someone my age" or "I'm too old to…" or "I'll be [age] when I can finally do it, so why bother?"

One-size-fits-all patterns for life are a thing of the past.

See if you can spot stereotypes and putdowns in your own talk. If you honestly don't want to do something or you have a real age or health restriction, you might be able to alter the activity to suit you today. Otherwise making excuses based on age for why you can't do something is short-changing yourself.

- "I'm too old to do it" could become "My age will affect how easy I'll find this, but it doesn't stop me unless I let it. It's never too late to give something a try." Get the support you need to make it possible.
- If you are saying "I'm too old to do that," think of people you know or search for people online who are doing what you want to do and are your age or older.
- If you see only the negatives of being older, you may find it hard to see the benefits. Appreciate the wide range of abilities and talents in this decade.
- When you hear that inevitable remark, "You don't look 60," one response is, "Sixty has many looks. Mine is one of them." How else could you respond?

Five

The Roof over Our Heads

We shape our dwellings, and afterwards, our dwellings shape us.

Winston Churchill

Our home. The secure base from which we venture out into the world, and to which we retreat to seek comfort and safety. We have practical ties to our home, but emotional ties, too, ties that can feel almost impossible to undo.

Our sixties are an important time to review the issues that affect our choice about housing. For many, our homes are our largest financial asset, and many of us plan to use home equity to finance retirement. We need to think about what kind of housing we can afford on our future income, especially if we still carry a mortgage.

We need space for our work and for new interests; we want rooms for visiting children and grandchildren; we may wish to live somewhere warm in winter; and we wonder how we'll manage in our home if our health fails down the road.

Do the homes we cling to give us what we really need or do they create more stress than they relieve?

In this chapter we look at the issues regarding the roof over our heads, the alternatives available to us, and whether our homes affect decisions about working, or conversely, how working affects choices about homes.

Homes R Lifestyle

We've been waiting for the time when we can pursue long-held interests—hobbies, income-generating ventures and travel, to name three, interests that may change the way we use our home.

William, previously a high school economics teacher, took up painting after he retired and turned part of his house into a studio. He'd sold some of his work and taken a few commissions. He and his wife could sell their house and move at any time, taking his painting supplies with him.

Karate wasn't new for Susan and her husband, but using their home as a karate studio and a B and B would be. They'd need a bigger home and a tourist location for those. Down the road, when they feel finished with the B and B and teaching karate, they could convert the whole area into a permanent rental suite.

Carl and Arlene had no plans to move from their 1100 sq. ft. bungalow. An incurable renovator, Carl had moved walls and the main floor bathroom several times. The latest reno gave them a large master bedroom with spa-like ensuite, powder room, and office on the main floor where they kept track of their several home-based businesses. When their two children and their families visited, they stayed in the renovated basement with its mini-kitchen, bedrooms, and technologically cool living area the grandchildren promptly claimed. He dedicated part of the garage to his hobby of refinishing cars.

An avid gardener who enjoyed year-round the vegetables she grew, Ruth vowed she would leave her home feet first.

PJ valued the privacy and quietness of her home, sure that an apartment building would not guarantee those.

Karen and Ole had lived for six years in an older mobile home they hauled north by barge and parked on a treed lot on an island on BC's central coast. They looked out over a wide bay, the fishing resort and marina where Ole worked, and the coastal mountain range. They also owned a patio home in the Comox Valley they returned to for part of every winter. When Ole quits work, they'll sell the mobile home to live in Comox permanently. They had a 33-foot trawler they moored at the marina, but expected they'd have to sell it when they moved south, ending their boating days, although Karen thought he'd be ecstatic if she agreed to buy a boat they could live on.

Linda and her husband had moved back home to a community on Nova Scotia's South Shore, financially burned after several years and two bad jobs in Ontario. She expected housing to be cheaper—that everything would be cheaper. The only thing lower was incomes. They bought a house on an acreage by a lake, with a large garden and a lot of firewood to haul, property it took them both to manage.

Will Home Equity Finance Our Future?

More than 40 percent of Canadians expect to use home equity to help finance living in retirement, according to a Bank of Montreal survey, quoted in the *Financial Post* in 2013.

Some will use their home's value to bridge any income shortfall, while others view their principal residence as a key component of their retirement income. That's because boomers have more money tied up in home equity than in other financial assets. What isn't clear is how we expect to live on home equity. Will we sell and downsize? Live on money from a reverse mortgage?

Boomers have had an enormous impact on housing in our lifetime and seen many changes in the market. As we began to buy houses in the 1970s, our demand pushed prices sky-high, while interest rates hit a torturous 21 percent in 1980. When unemployment soared in the eighties, foreclosures eroded neighbourhoods. Mortgage eligibility rules have loosened and tightened, and payment options have multiplied as a way to keep housing demand strong.

Our impact on housing will be felt once again around 2021, it's predicted, when the oldest boomers turn 76 and begin to sell single-family homes to buy smaller, more easily maintained housing. (Home ownership has traditionally declined after age 75). The demand for older, single-family houses won't keep up with the increasing supply, and prices will drop just as we want to draw out equity. In the meantime, a predicted nation-wide market adjustment could cause prices to drop. The result: Our equity may offer little to our retirement income at the same time as our demand for more user-friendly homes pushes up their cost. If we sell, timing the sale and purchase may be critical to our finances.

Selling and buying something smaller can reduce monthly housing costs. We can plough any profit from the sale into living expenses, travel, a bit of luxury, or investments.

Rhiannon, 63, wanted her equity to make money. Her two sons were on their own, and she felt no attachment to her suburban home. She wanted a more urban lifestyle, so she sold it and bought two 600-sq ft downtown condos. She moved into one, rented the other, and invested the rental income. Living in the city centre slashed the costs of commuting to her half-time job and of owning a car, as she walked to work and to concerts and plays. She planned to sell the condos and move to the west coast to be with her partner, who lived on his sailboat, and buy a cabin for herself.

Still Paying the Mortgage

Mortgages make up almost one-quarter of the debt we carry into our sixties, a Royal Bank survey found. Many of the mortgages are for more than half the value of the property, according to a TD Canada Trust survey, and some mortgages account for more than 75 percent of a home's value.

Those who have a mortgage feel more stress than those who don't own property (and presumably rent), said a McMaster University study. The stress of paying a mortgage may be worsened by being house poor—buying too much house on too little income. A one percent hike in the interest rate increases a mortgage payment by seven percent.

Our parents had their mortgages paid off in their sixties. How did we get into this predicament—if indeed it is a predicament?

The answers lie in housing costs in Canada, our confidence in rising house prices to better our financial position, and whether our lives have been turned upside down. We have been mobile, moving from regions with lower-priced housing to areas where we spend more to live in the same kind of house. We've traded up—homes today are three times larger than fifty years ago—while house prices have sky-rocketed. We've borrowed against our equity when interest rates were low to finance renovations or invest in other property or a business, risks we hoped would increase net worth, but that might not have. We've borrowed to finance our children's education and their business ventures. We've lost jobs and allowed mortgages to fall into arrears; and our marriages ended, forcing us to buy new homes.

When Gene and his wife separated, he kept the house. It was drenched in memories of happy family times, and his near-adult children could still live at home if they wanted to. He took out a second mortgage to buy out her half and to pay off their debts. When he retires at seventy, the first mortgage will be paid, but just. He'll be paying his second mortgage until he dies, he said with chagrin, and won't be able to do all the things he hoped to do in retirement.

The pain of Bunny's loss, the stress of selling his business and netting a mere $1,000 after years of building it, and moving away from the happy home where he'd died, left her unable to work. A month before she turned 50, she resigned and took an early pension. She just got by on the reduced pension for a couple of years while she made mortgage payments on the new house she bought in the city. She was pushed back to work when she took a hard look at paying a mortgage on a small income, all the while growing increasingly restless at home with little to do.

When David bought his house, he expected the final payment of his 25-year mortgage to come out of his first pension cheque. The date got pushed back after he was down-sized from his first job, and moved back once more when he lost his second job.

To Move or not to Move

Our sixties are a good time to move, says Davidson in *Leap!: What Will We Do for the Rest of Our Lives?* unless grown children have moved back home (more about that later). We've outgrown family-sized houses and are young enough to build a new life in a new place in our remaining active years.

However, fully half of us expect to stay in our current homes, the ones we raised our families in. The other half plan to move, although most will stay in the same town, city or area. We might move for social, lifestyle and financial reasons, but often, an unfortunate event—the death of a spouse, divorce or health crisis—forces us to move.

More than half of the movers plan to move to a smaller, single-detached home, said a *Globe and Mail* column. We want backyards and gardens; we also want deluxe features, a TD Canada Trust survey found. We aren't worried yet about whether we can climb stairs.

Our new home should be reasonably close to children, especially if we have grandchildren, and we'll go to great measures to be near them.

If her daughter moved to England for graduate school, Jan wanted to rent an apartment in the same city, taking advantage of her ability to work from home anywhere in the world. She also imagined living some place warmer in winter, perhaps Tuscany, with friends who would share the costs.

House or condo

Few of us want to move to a condominium although that depends on where we live—mega-city, urban, small town or rural. Even women are more likely to buy single-detached houses, with their maintenance demands, than a condo. We don't want to pay condo or strata fees, not understanding what fees provide, equating them with rent. I suspect our independent streak also comes into play. We don't want to give others control over our chief asset, and bad-news stories abound of the costs to remediate poorly built buildings, conflict between owners and boards, and condo values that don't keep pace with those of single-family houses. Fact is, home ownership presents different, not fewer, difficulties.

When Cora sold her small-city home and moved to the big city 110 miles south, she bought a condo a 10-minute walk from her daughter and grandchildren. Friends warned her that a condo was a bad choice: What if the stove needed replacing? What if she had to cough up extra money, a special assessment, for unforeseen repairs? Cora reasoned that someday she would need to buy a new stove in her house, not to mention do big-ticket improvements—a furnace and shingles.

We might not predict how prohibitive housing costs can suddenly become. *In Thunder Bay Keith was concerned about the pensioners who had been getting along until the city raised property taxes to make up for the industrial tax base lost in the 2008 recession. That many people could no longer afford their houses was an issue he wanted to address in his term as mayor.*

Aging in place

Aging in place, staying in our own homes and being cared for in them for as long as possible, will be the thrust of public policy for seniors' housing in the future, in part because building, staffing and operating publicly funded residential care facilities will be too costly. Aging in place works well when a person has a large network of informal support people, including children, in addition to formal supports. But many of us have had few children and at later ages, and it's likely they'll live too far from us and be engaged in their careers should we need care. The demand for home care assistants is expected to skyrocket, whether we age in place or in multi-resident facilities.

"The Newfoundland Ladies," a documentary on CBC's The Fifth Estate in the 2008-2009 season, offered a glimpse of in-home caregiving. For two-week stints, women from Newfoundland worked in Nova Scotia as live-in caregivers to physically disabled adults, and were relieved by a second woman who stayed for the following two weeks. Working half the year in two-week stretches and living at home the other half, each woman earned enough to support herself and her husband, their resourceful solution after Newfoundland's fisheries industry collapsed. Increasingly, live-in caregivers will come from south-east Asian countries, and many will need personal space in the home in which they work, one good reason to stay where we are. While ageing-in-place services will help us stay in our homes, as the years go by we'll become increasingly isolated within the suburbs we once sought. "More like prisoners," wrote researchers in one report I read.

It can take your car being on the fritz for a week to see how difficult it will be to live in the suburbs or small cities in our later years. For a winter week, when her car was in for repairs, Barb got a taste of the problems she'll face living in her city of 23,000 when she no longer drives. Without public transit, she felt stranded, because she didn't feel comfortable phoning someone to pick her up for routine errands or social events, or paying for a taxi. Barb wondered how long the benefits of staying in her home would outweigh the disadvantages, and what the tipping point would be.

The question of where to move had me flummoxed for several years. I was certain it would be a condo so I'd never again push a lawnmower or shovel snow, and smack-dab in the centre of a big Canadian city. But I also wondered about a less-costly Canadian city who-knows-where so I could invest some of my equity. I wanted to flee harsh winters and appreciate more of Canada's diversity. No city flashed a "Pick me" sign. Finally, my multiculturally rich city with top-notch healthcare, and family and friends close by, trumped change.

Moving permanently to some place warmer has perennial appeal. Four million Canadians are snowbirds—temporary migrants flocking each winter to mobile homes, condos and time-shares in the southern States, Mexico, Central America and the Caribbean. The US housing crisis of the early 2000s and our then strong dollar made ownership more affordable. Leveraging the equity in our Canadian home to pick up property at low prices to use as a get-away and investment added to our debt and cancelled some of our equity. A few dreams to own property in the tropics became nightmares: A sight-unseen condo that would never be built, an impossible-to-sell time-share that dropped in value while maintenance costs rose.

Selling

If our capital is tied up in more property than we use, if repairs and renovations are roof-high, and if the mortgage, taxes, utilities and maintenance are eating up more than 30 percent of our annual budget, it could be time to sell. However, leaving our home can be a difficult decision.

Place attachment is the name for the panic and loss we feel when we think about selling our home. Imagine hundreds of strings tying you to your home: Decades of memories within four walls; the trees and flowers you lovingly tended; the view from every window; friendly neighbours; the marks etched on the wall to measure kids' growth. You untie those strings. Then there are countless decisions about the mountain of things you have accumulated—what to keep, what to give to the kids or charity, what to throw away. Besides downsizing, the process of searching, buying, selling, packing, renovating, moving and settling in seems overwhelming. The stress inherent in moving can even affect our health.

When I contemplated selling and moving, I was confused about which decision to make first, since every decision seemed to impinge on every other. Occasionally I felt stalled by fear, and cleared it with a good cry. I sweated the decision of how much of my equity to put into a condo, how much to invest, how much to spend over how many years. (Two financial advisers suggested as many options). I couldn't imagine feeling relief and excitement at opportunities that might come my way. The intensity of my emotions was put into perspective when a friend said that as we age, we have fewer opportunities to feel intensely. A decision as large and complex as moving stirs up emotional turmoil such as we felt in our youth.

It takes time to build a new life in a new neighbourhood. *It took Karen a couple of years before her home on BC's central coast felt like home. After I moved, a friend chirpily said, "You're building a new life in your condo." "I suppose so. But I don't know what that life looks like. I have to grow into it, whatever it is," I agreed cautiously.*

A cost-benefit analysis can be useful as you weigh the options in a decision. In your analysis list the logical advantages and disadvantages of each option. Then, since emotions play an important role in decision making, acknowledge how you feel about each advantage and disadvantage. Words such as scared, intrigued, secure, sad, excited, and relieved may apply.

What we may find difficult to acknowledge is that selling our home and moving are an admission of something we prefer not to talk about. This could be our last move.

Own or rent

Home ownership is synonymous with being grown-up, and a single detached house is the responsible place to park and grow money. Ownership is a source of pride, enabling us to portray an image that says we're financially alright. Ownership guarantees we are king in our own castle, can pound nails into walls or paint them a vibrant green, and keep housing costs in our own hands. That appears to be the common view among Canadians.

Seven out of 10 Canadians own their own home, though not all are mortgage-free. But, not everyone wants to, nor can afford to, own their own home. Renting rather than owning a home is a good financial strategy when the housing market destabilizes, something that is predicted in Canada (although prices continue to rise in some Canadian cities). But people rent for other reasons, a common one being altered finances after divorce.

When Jan said that she chooses to rent, and would continue to do so, it gave me pause. After she divorced, buying a house seemed out of the question. She reasoned that no bank would give a mortgage to a single, self-employed, 60-year old woman in the Montreal neighbourhood she preferred to raise her daughter in. So, having decided that her security lay in her talents and abilities, Jan invested her share from the sale of the marital home and began to rent. She was considering renting a smaller, less expensive home when her daughter finished university and left home. Her choice was about her personal circumstances, but it also reflects a regional bias toward renting. In some parts of Canada, including Montreal, renting is viewed as an equal, not lesser, option to owning.

Being a renter in Victoria where rents are "hideously high" left Sally feeling insecure and unsettled. Twice she had to move out of buildings to make way for renovations. When we talked, she was house sitting—a good way to cut housing costs—but she was about to move once more, now that the house-sit was over.

Julie and her husband, who was determined to farm, had both worked in town, she waitressing for years to plough her earnings into the farm. When she left her marriage at 48, she took her personal belongings, but to mollify him—she believed that the abuse would continue after she left—she signed over to him her interest in everything they owned. At first she rented. A few years later, she moved to northern Manitoba and bought a house, which she later sold when she moved in with a new partner.

Jim had rented since his divorce as well, but was intrigued with communal living and the increasing number of co-housing societies in Canada.

Co-housing societies range from urban to rural, mixed-age to similarly-aged owners, families to singles. Some societies lean toward car sharing and green lifestyles. Communities may have a mix of closely spaced houses and apartments or one large, many-bedroomed house. Residents often share common areas, a weekly meal and household chores. Co-housing communities operate on consensus decision-making and living in close proximity, so they aren't for everyone. But they can give the financial security of ownership while resolving some of the issues of social isolation and lack of practical support, common issues of aging.

Borrowing against equity: reverse mortgages

Expecting we will want money in our later years and be reluctant to sell our homes, lenders developed reverse mortgages, also called lifetime or CHIP (Canadian Home Income Plan) mortgages. CHIP loans allow us to borrow from 40 to 50 (one website quoted 55) percent of our home's net value (market value less debt attached to it), and not make payments as long as we live in it. The loan is due when we move or sell.

I checked out online how such a deal would benefit me. Default settings on drop-down menus showed an annual lending rate of 3.75 percent and a projected 4 percent annual increase in property value. Those values seemed marginally attractive. If they stayed the same for 20 years, I'd be well-off, sort of, when I moved to a seniors' residence in my late eighties. But if the value of my house only slowly increased (the predicted scenario), flattened or lost value (both possible), and the interest rate increased (we're told it's inevitable), I could effectively transfer all my equity to the lender in less than 15 years if I never made a payment on the loan, likely before I would be ready to sell my home. Paying the interest costs annually would at least preserve equity.

Some financial experts say that the earliest age we should think about taking out a reverse mortgage is our seventies. Others say we should spend our equity, implying that we won't care if we're broke when we're older. The question is whether to spend equity on pleasure and perhaps necessities now or save it for living expenses later. Several years ago a Member of Parliament purportedly said that reverse mortgages are good only when you don't like your children and want to leave them nothing. The ads are tempting. Each of us will decide according to our own priorities.

To reduce expenses, we can pay off the mortgage or sell and buy a less expensive home. To increase income, we can borrow against our equity. There's another option, deriving actual income from our home.

PUTTING OUR HOMES TO WORK

The emotional and symbolic value we give our homes bears no relation to its dollar value, and real estate prices reflect their value in a regional sphere only. Homes that work for us add additional value, in that household expenses to operate home-based businesses can reduce the income tax we pay, and homes can be a source of active income when they are themselves the business.

One of the five must-haves in homes bought today is a home office, a Better Homes and Garden Real Estate survey found. That can be as simple as an unused bedroom converted to an office or as elaborate as a pre-construction designated office suite with its own entrance and bathroom.

Boomers are incorporating offices in their home at the same rate as younger age groups, as they turn to de-centralized employment and self-employment in the next career stage.

As self-employeds, we need office space and equipment to write, teach, consult and operate service businesses. *Jim needed a dedicated space for his office as well as space to temporarily store the collectibles he sold on eBay. Carl needed space for tools and supplies for renovation projects, and Arlene ran her landscaping and book-keeping businesses from their home office. Cora taught, wrote and edited from the bedroom-cum-office in her condo. Jan wrote at home, and Sally did her on-line editing contracts from home. Mary operated her communications consultant business from her home, going into the office one day a week to stay connected to the organization. Josée needed a home office and a large, dedicated space to teach yoga; her husband needed an office for his work as an engineering consultant. The house they bought and renovated gave them two offices and a studio in the basement. Terri taught graduate students on-line from her home office 450 kilometres from the university where she had previously taught on campus. Stephen worked from his near-Toronto home as the regional representative of a company in Quebec.*

By the time they're both 65 Susan and her husband planned to open a bed and breakfast in a British Columbia city known for cultural and outdoor tourism.

They would sell their prairie home and take on a mortgage to buy the new property, designing it to include the B and B and space to offer karate courses. Alternatively, they might provide guest accommodation in summers and rent rooms to college students in winters. Their venture would need to bring in enough income to pay the mortgage and give them a small profit to make their effort worthwhile, but her pension would cover the rest of their needs.

Our home as the business is a bold move. For many, self-employment and operating a small business will be a learning curve.

Women and Home Ownership

Women's ownership of homes has come a long way since we were young. Then, women didn't routinely put their name on a property title, and only one-half of a woman's income was included in family earnings in a couple's application for a mortgage, regardless of how much she earned or the number of years she had worked.

Owning a home on their own can worry some women. You might think women's fear of becoming homeless shopping cart ladies was long past, but apparently not, says *Women, Power and Money*, a 2013 Allianz Life study. Forty-nine percent of women, even high-income earners in that US study, said they feared homelessness. It's a cultural fear we've absorbed through generations, although it's not well-founded today. *"I've had dreams of being out on the street with a basket with all my goods, but it's never actually happened,"* said Mary, who had been self-employed nearly all her working life.

Women head 38 percent of Canadian households. More women live alone at a younger age than did older generations, and almost half of older women living alone are home owners, although a greater proportion are widowed as compared to divorced or never married. Owning a home on their own or paying the rent themselves pushes some women to work longer.

In retirement women's post-employment earnings are lower than men's, so they have less money to go toward housing. They may need to look to different housing arrangements, and if they live alone, they may need to be even more creative when it comes to housing, to avoid spending a huge chunk of their income on housing. *"Why not share?"* Bev asked.

SHARE YOUR SPACE

Sharing our living space with people we don't know isn't something we Canadians like to do. In Europe, however, experiments in social housing are sprouting up to help older people stay in their homes and to give young people an affordable place to live.

In France, older home owners charge a modest monthly rent to younger people in exchange for practical help and social support. In *LinkAges*, a similar program in England, young adults offer practical help in exchange for a place to live. In both programs participants are screened and matched according to interests and needs. Formal agreements are drawn up, and sponsoring agencies monitor the matches. It appears that on this side of the Atlantic, we have do-it-yourself versions only.

Debbie, 58, liked living in her suburban house, but found that there was too much solitude. So, she signed up to provide room and board to young adult international students attending the university's English-language school. She reported the modest income on her income tax return and put the slim profit toward her mortgage.

Secondary suites are common in older neighbourhoods of Canadian cities, and the numbers will only grow as municipalities prioritize increasing the density of housing in central neighbourhoods to check urban sprawl and reduce the costs of developing and servicing suburbs. Grant money is often available to help home-owners renovate basements or build back-yard cottages for secondary suites. The HGTV program *Income Property* (watch past episodes on youtube.com) makes secondary suites look like a smart thing to have.

The house I bought in the early 1990s had a basement mother-in-law suite. I spent more than I expected to upgrade it, but when it was done I relished banking money I had done little to earn and appreciated having someone in the house when I was away. In 20 years, I had two tenants I wish I hadn't and many college students I enjoyed getting to know.

Two recent and popular online home-sharing options—Airbnb and Vrbo (Vacation Rental by Owner)—provide homeowners with other options to make extra income from short-term rental of space in their homes.

With more adult children not leaving home or moving back to their parents' home with their own children after their marriage and / or job ends, it's possible that home-sharing with our kids and grandchildren could become a permanent arrangement. That can take many forms.

Donald had been retired for two years when his and Claire's 30-year old daughter moved back home with her 5-year old son, after Donald rescued her from a terrible marriage. They decided to support her as much as possible so she could build a life as a single parent. Together they planned a course of action which started with Donald going back to work at 64. He thought about returning to his former employer—he'd managed a hardware store—but there were no positions close to home and he wanted something with less responsibility. When a friend told him that the car rental agency he worked for needed someone, Donald jumped at it. It was a perfect fit—he liked the bustling atmosphere and meeting people. Their daughter enrolled in a college program, and Claire took care of their grandson. "It's taken a bit of adjusting. Sometimes I want to give my daughter advice about how she disciplines her son, but Claire reminds me to stay out. We'll probably want to help her once she's working and they move out, so I might work five more years. I'm just glad we're able to help her," Donald said.

Doug's youngest son, at 30, lived with his parents while his house was being built. Doug's mother, who was 85, had lived with them for 12 years. Their grandson often lived with them whenever his parents were away.

The flip side is moving in with our kids, which might not appeal to many. *Mary's daughter had offered her a granny suite in her home halfway across the country should Mary need one in the future. That future was too far off for her to accept the offer, but she hadn't ruled it out. Linda had told her three children that she'd move in with them if she ran out of money. "They all said, 'Not a problem.' I wouldn't move into the same house with them. I'd move into a house behind them or over a garage, and I wouldn't do it as long as I had money of my own," Linda said.*

A Last Word

Our home may be our nest or retirement nest egg, our refuge or castle, a money pit or money-maker. It may be the reason we're still working, our workspace or a source of income. One day it may be our personal long-term care facility. We may consider our homes disposable or never sell them. We may look at living with children with pleasure or panic. Whatever it is, our sixties are a time to evaluate whether our home serves us now and how it will serve us as we age. In the next chapter we look at how boomers will remake the last frontier of life—retirement.

Activity: Review the roof over your head

A home gives us shelter, supports lifestyle and stores memories. If we own our home, it's also a financial asset to be used for emergencies or as an inheritance. These questions may help you think about whether your home suits your needs today and in the future, and whether its costs are pushing you to work or whether it can help provide income.

Does your lifestyle point to less home upkeep, less financial outlay?

- Is your home essential to your quality of life, interests and hobbies?

Do you have more money in home equity or in financial assets?

In what way can your home be a source of income?

- Laneway housing, granny suite or room rental
- Reverse mortgage
- Home-based business
- Equity converted to cash. Or, sell, buy a less expensive home and invest the balance.

Is renting an option?

Do the costs of living in your home eat up more than 30 percent of your income?

- Add all costs: mortgage payment, property taxes, normal maintenance and repairs, unusual maintenance and repairs, utilities, insurance and renovations.
- The "shadow cost" of your home is the income you're not earning on the investment you'd make — assuming you'd invest the proceeds — if you sold your home.

Can you grow old in your home or will you eventually need to move?

- What circumstance (infirmity, etc.) would force you to move?
- Do you know what you'd do if you became semi-dependent or dependent?
- Will your locale support or isolate you in old age?
- Are proximity to health services, cultural activities and adult children a consideration?

What would you do with your possessions if you moved? Can you imagine which of these five categories they fit in: keep, sell, give to family and friends, donate, and throw out?

What do you feel when you think about leaving your home?

We need to be shrewd, even hard-headed, to alter our housing lifestyle, to take risks and foresee long-term issues while holding on to memories.

Six

Re/Working Retirement

Two weeks is about the ideal length of time to retire.

A GOOD AGE, ALEX COMFORT, 1976

*T*hroughout my working years I assumed I'd retire at about 65, much like my mother and her generation had done. I was in my late fifties when I realized that wasn't going to happen. I had been self-employed for 12 years while working part-time, a lifestyle I planned to continue indefinitely. Retirement as I had imagined it was nowhere in sight. Eventually I started to call myself quasi-retired. I might look like I was retired (writing is an invisible occupation; for all people knew I was vegging out in front of TV or reading a good book), but I didn't have the signature attribute of a retired person—a passive income large enough to live on.

I'm among the million or so front-end boomers in Canada who have celebrated our sixtieth birthday and are facing our seventieth. Like many of us, I'm wondering about my prospect for retirement and trying to figure out if I'll ever retire.

When Do We Retire?

To some retirement is elusive. To others it's undesirable. You read about how finances make retirement elusive in the chapter Show Me the Money, but other factors push us to retire.

We retire when the benefits of retirement are greater than the benefits of working. How much we like or need to work, how much non-working income we have, how much taking it easy we can take, the state of our health, our interests, and subtle or not-so-subtle pressures from family, the workplace and the culture all figure into the decision to retire. In times past, disability and illness often pushed people to retire. They retired when they had enough resources, usually a combination of money and family support, to quit—family support usually meant living with children. Only the well-off could actually afford to retire, and a person who received a pension was expected to quit working entirely.

We're told that our years between 65 and 80 are our golden years, and that retirement is the best way to spend these years (before old age imposes limitations), as a just reward for a lifetime of labour. Yet we could live 20 to 25 percent of our lives in this non-working nirvana; that forces us to re-assess how to live these later years.

As early as our late forties and early fifties we began to think about working in our later years, long before the 2008 recession ravaged our retirement savings. You will recall the 1999 AARP survey that asked U.S. boomers about their attitude toward retirement and retirement savings behaviour and then grouped respondents into five work-retirement scenarios. The 2001 people were called the *strugglers,* who had no savings and needed to work; the *anxious,* who would work to supplement scant savings, pensions and social security; the *self-reliants,* who would work at least part-time because work gave intrinsic rewards; the *traditionalists,* who would work for money, liked to work, and would start a business; and the *enthusiasts,* who wouldn't work at all. Perhaps you identify with one of those groups.

The people you will meet in this chapter are reworking their ideas about retirement and creating a variety of ways to make the most of these golden years. Although I didn't start this book intending to talk to people who were retired, before long, I learned that the retired-and-back-at-work and the not-going to-retire had many similarities. In the end, I wanted to know how everyone defined retirement, what they considered to be a good age to retire, and what they expected to do in retirement.

What Retirement Means

Retirement has always meant the opposite of work—a complete leave-taking from work. Perhaps that's why we think of retirement as a passive and unproductive life stage with few ways to use skills and talents. Today, we can retire and work part-time, phase in retirement (20 to 30 percent of those eligible for retirement choose to phase into it), semi-retire, intermittently retire, and my take, quasi-retire. We can think of full retirement at the extreme end of a continuum with full-time work at the opposite end, with greater and lesser amounts of non-work and work in between.

Here's what people said

I asked everyone what their thoughts about retirement were.

Bev was influenced by the ideas Richard Bolles expressed in his book The Three Boxes of Life. We spend 25 years in learning, 40 in working and 15 in retirement, in discreet, orderly steps, but we should strive for more balance. Bev decided to unlock the predictable steps and 'mix it up'. Work would need to fund a very long period of her retirement—her genes could take her into her 90s—so she would need more money than she had when we talked. Bev planned to work full-time until about 68 using the master's degree in professional communication she had earned at 57, doing contract or consulting work to help people in work groups develop communication skills. Those skills, she maintained, are at the heart of everything we do. Her eventual retirement could mean travelling, but she looked forward to having time to cook healthier meals, being more physically active, and spending more time with friends and family.

After retiring from teaching, Ruth caught her breath for a few months and then took a couple of low-paying jobs, demonstrating food products at the supermarket and serving food and drink at the high-flyer lounge at the airport, jobs which forced her to spend almost all she earned on massage and chiropractors to alleviate the pain of physically demanding work. When a former teaching buddy suggested she try a vehicle remarketing company, she found her niche, working eight shifts a month driving cars into the auction ring, and one day a week in the concession, weaving in golf trips to Palm Springs and other vacations. But to Ruth, retirement boiled down to being free to go to the bank in the middle of the day and not putting in long hours as a teacher.

Apparently leaving a top-notch senior management position at 56—because the changes you proposed to restructure the company eliminated your executive job—makes you retired in other people's eyes, no matter what you go on to do after you leave. Stephen said, "When I left, I wrote on my LinkedIn page 'In transition'. I would run into people who would say, 'So, how do you enjoy retirement?' It made my stomach turn, because I wasn't retired." His downtime was the few months he spent figuring out what to do next and putting plans in place. To Stephen retirement meant "…re-inventing myself on a regular basis, maybe a constant transition to new experiences."

"Retirement is a relief," Gwen said, although she, office manager and bookkeeper, and her husband, an accountant, had left their bookkeeping and accounting business while they still enjoyed it. "Had it not been for tax time, when you work day and night for four months, we could have kept on doing accounting," she said, even though they had wound down five years earlier by reducing the number of personal tax returns they did. But Gwen was still working, regularly helping her son in his bookkeeping business and her daughter in her home staging business, although neither paid her.

As long as Mary could write she didn't see retirement in her future, even though she would quit her nearly full-time job when she earned enough through writing and publishing fiction. Then, Mary would be so busy she wouldn't think of herself as retired.

Cora defined retirement as resigning from a full-time job and moving from employment income to pension income, between ages 55 and 65. But "to stop working, to stop contributing to life and receiving from life, I don't think there is an age or an end to that, that there's a retirement to that aspect of things," she said.

After Cora retired, she earned a certificate in adult and continuing education to add to her credentials to teach adults. She had always wanted to retire from teaching while she still loved it, but in her last 10 years in the classroom she watched several colleagues carried away by depression, stress, and one by a heart attack, coworkers who didn't finish teaching so much as be torn from it. The year she turned 55 her pension reached its max, and for the first time in 30 years, on the first day of school, Cora thought, "Do we have to do this again?" instead of wondering what the year would be like. A friend urged her to retire, but she fretted, equating retirement with starvation." "...like I was still back in 1967 when I thought I'd never collect CPP". Believing that she had to work to have an income, she immediately took tutoring jobs, creating a work-life full of little pieces. Time spent pondering what else she wanted to do with her life shifted her attitude. "I could make choices based on what I wanted, instead of what was necessary. It was a freedom I'd never had before."

"People usually think when you get to this point [close to retirement age] that you're tailing off, that you've done what you wanted to do," said Elle. "I'm like many writers of the same generation who are saying, 'Wow, I've got so much to do yet.'" Elle didn't see an end-date to her work other than "... in the sense that you can get Canada Pension, all these things....I don't know what retirement is. I think the baby boomer word for retirement is you leave one job where you get a pension, perhaps, and move on to another, something you enjoy doing more."

PJ had taken an early retirement package at 46, knowing such packages wouldn't be around much longer. Over the next decade she did various jobs, until she landed one that fit her to a T. At 62 and working full-time, PJ didn't have a clear picture of what she'd do with herself everyday if she wasn't working. Certainly retirement would mean not getting up and going to work every day, but that could mean a lot of empty hours and endless TV watching. She would have to organize her life to fill the time, to do some traveling, reading, cooking, and playing mahjong with friends—things she never had time to do while she was working.

Karen and Ole's sale of their house and trucking company wasn't retirement so much as a change of pace. They couldn't live their preferred lifestyle for long on the money from the sales, so they moved to BC's central coast where Ole began to work full-time and Karen pieced together part-time and seasonal jobs. In the future, when they no longer enjoyed working or if health dictated that one of them should quit, they would partly retire and move back to the Comox Valley where Ole would work part-time to keep busy. Retirement would mean pulling back if they could no longer afford to maintain and moor their much-loved boat when they left the central coast. They also hoped to roam across Canada and the States in their truck and camper.

Travel and retirement are almost synonymous, so much so that seniors' travel will become a lucrative target of the travel industry in the coming years. It seems that money, a spouse and travel are inter-twined.

Gene had dreamed of traveling, perhaps to Greece and across Canada. Newspaper images—a couple in front of beautiful buildings—shouted retirement to him. Gene's reaction: "Shit, I'll never be able to do that. I feel a bit sad. I don't have the money to do that and I don't have the partner to do it with. But I still have a bit of a dream to do something like that, just once. I thought by the time I reached retirement the house would be paid for and we'd be sailing, but life decided otherwise."

To Gene retirement was a double-edged sword. Why quit work while he was still learning, enjoying work's camaraderie, feeling respected in the community and making a difference? He'd never thought that just because you're 65, you retired. He was a little afraid of what he'd do with himself in winter's long months—he'd had a taste of not working when he was off work for a knee replacement in his early 60s. "It did something to me, those three or four months of not working, almost demoralized me." His pictures of retirement were volunteering at the food bank, maybe working part-time. "Maybe I'll get a gym pass to get in shape or join a seniors' swim club. Meet other people."

Before Carl retired, Arlene had a dismal vision of his retirement. She would take care of him, he wouldn't help around the house, he'd always be in her space, and he wouldn't find very much to do, other than what he'd done before retirement, now as a private contractor. A year after he retired, she said, "He's doing real things [driving school bus, renovating other people's homes as a business]. He's not just hiding in his garage." She hadn't thought they'd travel much, that all their talking prior to his retirement talk had been just talk. So it came as a surprise that they were so busy with their part-time jobs and businesses that they didn't have much time to travel, and it didn't matter. "Freedom 55—they show where you're paddling in some ocean in the tropics. I never believed we'd be financially able to do it."

"I really wish I knew what retirement means," Jan said. "I have a feeling that retirement has a much straighter meaning for people who've always been employed in somebody's office, because there's a cut-off. One day you're working and one day you're not. For self-employed people it's different. Retirement means, obviously, that I get QPP at a certain point. Retirement will be a gradual process." She never expected to retire with a pension. "I'd been at [an international magazine] for a year. The practice was that after you'd been there a year you were to start contributing to the company plan. When I was around 30, my boss asked me, 'How come you haven't signed up yet?' I looked at him and said, in my most polite voice but firmly, 'I have no intention of being here when I'm 65.' I didn't know it until I said it, but it was true."

"Retirement is like being plunged into another world. That's dreadful. It's like an iron door shutting off the whole of your previous life. I think it's very bad for your mental health. I will never retire," said Sally. "Maybe I'm not realistic, but I always thought things would take care of themselves," she said, calling herself "a child of the sixties." Working a lifetime in one organization would have made retirement a cut-and-dried-deal, but it would have been a major hurdle for her. Besides, Sally was too busy travelling and living to contemplate retirement.

Norm hinted at a belief that may be common, but isn't often stated. "People who are retired are probably people who grew up," he said. The implication is that those who had had steady jobs with a pension and worked until they were pensionable had lived their lives in a more mature manner than those who had changed jobs and arrived in their sixties with little or no pension. Like many boomers, Norm had chosen another path, working at jobs without pensions, and changing jobs.

The zeitgeist is a freer kind of career building and an approach to work that's less stressful, as Elle suggested. People can leave one job, perhaps with a pension, and move to another more enjoyable and less intense job. Courses such as "Don't Retire, Re-wire" are sprouting up to introduce us to the idea of continuing our careers.

Is 70 the New 65?

Many boomers will say, "I'm working on the Freedom 85 plan."

We grew up with the idea that 65 is the ideal age to retire. The age of eligibility for OAS at 65 helped establish the notion, as did collective agreements between unions and workers' associations and their employers, which typically made retirement at 65 mandatory (some agreements stipulated 60). But mandatory retirement has all but been retired, except where it is a *bona fide* requirement of the occupation, so the average retirement age has been freed up to float.

In the 40-plus years since we started to work the retirement age has fallen. It dropped to its lowest ever, 61.2 years, around the turn of the millennium, largely as a consequence of the downsizing purges and early retirement packages of the 1990s. Public service workers, many in their fifties, were big winners in the downsizing bonanza. Corporate employees were also lured from work by generous financial and pension packages, but they were older, on average, than public service workers. Meanwhile, self-employed people continued to work until 65, and employees in the private sector retired at an age between them and the youngest retirees. Many of those early retirees went on to establish second careers.

Nearly seven out of ten Canadians quit work before they plan to. Forty percent of those retire because of personal health problems. Others retire early because they can't find work after being laid off or because family members are ill.

The average retirement age is on the rise again, largely in response to economic conditions and government policies. The recent increase in the penalty for receiving CPP each year prior to age 65 and the increased benefit for beginning to receive it after 65 will increase the average age of retirement, although that change is meant to give the CPP pot time to grow and ensure its future sustainability with the large number of boomers drawing benefits.

The average age of retirement is pushing toward 70. Our emotional attachment to work and our personal finances will exert the greatest pressure upward. Many a boomer might say, perhaps wryly as they reflect on the elusive nature of retirement, "I'm working on the Freedom 85 plan."

How much taking it easy can you take?

*I don't think I'm ever going to retire. I can't sit
on a beach in Florida and do nothing.*

Keith

You've worked hard; you deserve to take it easy. It's time to enjoy life's pleasures. That's the prevailing belief.

But, how much taking it easy can you take? Just because you've always enjoyed weekends or holidays doesn't mean you're going to like a long work-free retirement. Furthermore, balance in life isn't achieved by tacking 25 years of leisure onto 40 years of labour. For many people the things that leaven our life while we work aren't enough to be the focus of life when we quit.

Cross-stitching, making cards, scrapbooking, and taking cruises weren't enough for Bunny. Before she resigned at 50, her boss had asked her if she'd consider being groomed for the boss's position when she retired. Bunny rejected the offer and quit, thinking she'd never work again, even though she'd long had a gloomy vision of retiring at 55 and dying within six months. Once at home she landscaped her new house, ran errands for her mother and aunt, took up quilting, but hardly saw friends. "That fall and winter I just about went crazy," she said, describing the cabin fever, the lingering trauma of her husband's death, and too much time on her hands. The next summer she kept thinking, "It's going to be winter and I'm going to be locked in this house," and started to panic. Her financial adviser suggested she get a part-time job. The job slowly grew to five days a week. If she was going to work full-time, she might as well go back to government where she'd get more money, she reasoned. Once there, HR asked her how long she planned to work. 'I have no idea, but I'll try to give you six months' notice,' she replied. "What's the point of retirement? I'd be in the position of being home and not having enough to do...I can't get my head around retirement. I've worked since I was 18. To suddenly not have that job, I don't know how I'd function." When Bunny eventually retires, she will need to be very busy, mentally and physically active and volunteering.

The process of retiring and retirement can be hard on us. *Death shortly after retirement is a problem in the police profession, Keith said.* "I encourage people to keep going. That's what I would say to anyone contemplating retiring. Keep going, be productive, even as a volunteer. Life is too short. Keep your life going. I think, in my profession as a police officer, I saw a lot of people retire and then die within a year…one guy died the day after he retired. In policing, it's ridiculous. I don't know if it's just the policing profession, but I think it's the high stress of that job and then doing nothing."

In *Claiming Your Place at the Fire: Living the Second Half of your Life on Purpose* (2004), Richard Leider wrote, "Retirement is a role-less role…. Retirement [as it's conceived today] can turn purposeful lives into tragedies."

Alex Comfort, in *A Good Age* (1976), proposed that we reject leisure as the goal of retirement, maintaining that, "Two weeks is about the ideal length of time to retire." He wrote that what we need is "dignity, money, proper medical services, and useful work."

Retirement—a right, entitlement or privilege?

Retirement is a social value to be respected, says the Canadian government's National Seniors Council, in the Report on the Labour Force Participation of Seniors and Near Seniors, and Intergenerational Relations. Although we value an active and affordable retirement, our background may influence whether we think retirement is a right, entitlement, or privilege.

Retirement is a right, not merely a privilege, Keith said, although early retirement began to feel like a right in the 1990s. "I think we owe it to people who have worked hard all their life to retire and do nothing, not to stand on their feet and work when they're 75." That belief may be a reflection of Keith's background in a unionized environment, where the majority of employees have pensions. That said, he also believed that retirement is about being productive, keeping going, finding a way to use the skills and adjust work to fit this later life stage.

The expectation to retire reflects a belief in retirement as an entitlement. *David had always believed that retirement was a predictable part of his life plan;*

his union job had guaranteed a pension, and the culture of the 1970s taught it. After his buy-out at 40 and second lay-off 13 years later, David knew there would be no retirement in his future. He was having trouble shaking the attitude that you work hard and then you retire. "When I started with the railway, I knew I was going to get a pension in 30 years and life would be wonderful. Everybody in the office, to a man, would say it was a retirement job. It shocked the hell out of everybody when they laid off 1400 people in one swat. Then I got this other job, and I thought, 'I'm going to work for this guy until one of us croaks.' My only concern was he would retire and I'd be stuck. Then I got laid off again. That really sucked."

It's the element of choice that separates having to work and wanting to work, positions that can feel miles apart. *Doug didn't want to quit doing what he was doing [in politics]; what he wanted was the free time and freedom retirement gave.* "In the back of my mind, I know I always have the option of not working if I really don't want to," he said. He believed everyone should have the option to retire about the time they're 60 or 62. "Having the option for the last five years [of our work-life] gives us a mental well-being, which is more important than money," he said. Doug felt badly for people in their 60s in low paying jobs, especially physical jobs, who wouldn't have enough to retire on and who had to keep working. They were among the population being targeted in a poverty reduction and inclusion strategy he was planning.

Cora often thought about what life was going to be like for women who, like her, were on their own and who had to make choices about what to do after retirement. "Given the precarious economic situation in the world, I think so many people could be at a tipping point where if you don't have enough, life could be difficult. They end up not being able to make the choices they'd like to make. I feel particularly privileged and happy that I've been able to make choices to allow me to have the life of travel and writing that I want. I've been able to move to be very close to my grandchildren," she said.

Retirement is also thought of as a social obligation. "We're almost conditioned to think if you don't retire by 65 and make room for young people coming up, you're a bad person," Doug said.

A contrasting belief is revealed in the pressure to retire that comes from the way organizations view older workers. Some see older workers through a depreciation lens, a view that believes the value of older workers climbs early in their career, maintains a high level until mid-life and then begins to decline, dropping to its lowest at a pre-determined older age. Employers with this belief decrease their investment in older workers, providing fewer training dollars, failing to re-design jobs to suit them, and providing regular pensions and early retirement packages to entice them to leave. Other organizations see employees through a conservation lens, believing that employees contribute to the organization regardless of age. These organizations invest in older workers and develop ways to retain them, believing that doing so helps them contribute to the organization.

If retirement were a right, we would have compulsory, universal adequate pension programs. But we don't (OAS is social security, not a pension), and there's no indication we ever will. The Canadian belief is that retirement is a desired way to spend one's later years, and that people shoulder most of the responsibility for creating some sort of retirement for themselves at about 65.

That leaves privilege, a non-working lifestyle some have through social status, special immunity, or wealth. Retirement is a privilege many (although decreasing numbers of) people in developed countries enjoy. Worldwide, it is a rare privilege—only two out of ten people retire.

Activity

What is your opinion? Is retirement a right, privilege or entitlement?

Early Retirement and the Freedom-55 Virus

Who could have escaped the airwaves laden with the financial industry's freedom 55 campaign and stories of gravy-rich early retirement packages? Boomers are the first generation to ever be seduced by early retirement.

Early retirement packages as a quick-fix restructuring tool and a solution for high unemployment rates had serious consequences. They made the unemployment rate artificially low in the short term. In the long-term, the sheer number of early retirements created a labour shortage and a financial burden on the public purse and pension funds. They also created an unrealistic expectation and reinforced the notion that older workers are dispensable. Perhaps worst of all, they eroded a healthy attitude to work in later life.

Norm worked in the insurance industry during the Freedom 55 campaign, launched in 1989. He said "Freedom 55! We started to get into that dream. We thought the thing to do was to retire instead of getting up every day and going to work, whatever the work is. And maybe the work is in retirement. The whole thing was based on fear that you're not going to have enough money. You're not going to live. You're not going to do this. So that's one thing I didn't like." Norm's friends, the retired ones who are happy, are working very hard on, say, the library or hospital board. "So our work just changes," he said.

"I know well that Freedom 55 feeling. That was always my intention, 55 and I'm out of there, but I couldn't have afforded it even if I wanted to," said Doug. Throughout his career he had taken advantage of the deferred salary program, working four years at 80 percent of his salary and taking the fifth year off while receiving 80 percent.

Carl was also bitten by the Freedom 55 bug. He had forecast that the numbers would crunch just right and they'd have enough money to pay the bills without working when he was 62. At 55 he grabbed one, predicting that generous early retirement packages would soon disappear.

Some occupations, such as policing, build in early retirement. *Keith had thought about retiring at 50, but it was a better idea financially, to stick around for a while longer. Although a police officer can now stay on until 65—the age barrier is now gone—he still saw it as a young person's job.*

Many boomers will experience more than one retirement.

After the company he had worked at for many years was sold, Rick began to see that the new owners were pushing him out. He asked what they were offering. Early retirement, fifteen months' pay, and benefits for a year. He sought legal advice and was told that anything more would come at a cost. Rick had already decided he'd work 'til he was 70 to keep sane and because he and his wife couldn't travel in retirement due to her disability. In the year after he took the package, he worked on-and-off for a temp agency, prepared his resume and formulated a plan for what was next. Then he landed work as a courier—a job filled by many workers who stayed on past 65. He said, "When I get up and don't want to go to work anymore, say when I'm 68, I'll quit, on my own terms."

Seven Retirement Myths Debunked

Myth: *Retirement is a time to take up something new.*
Fact: We may try out a new activity and put a lot of time into it at first, but we tend not to keep it up. Usually, we carry on doing the same things we've always done. Putting something off until retirement usually means we aren't going to do it.

Myth: *We can and should save enough to retire.*
Fact: Many people have no extra money to save. We have had no idea how much we needed to save to fund decades of retirement.

Myth: *Retirement is a predictable life stage.*
Fact: Retirement is a social construction of the late 19th century, enjoyed by people in the industrialized world.

Myth: *Retirement is irreversible.*
Fact: Today, people move from work to retirement and back again, more than once.

Myth: *Older people in the workforce are a barrier to younger people getting a start to their career.*
Fact: Boomers leaving the workforce will create tremendous gaps in the labour force and a significant brain drain of knowledge, leadership and experience. Furthermore, it's predicted that boomers' reduced spending in retirement will contribute to an economic slowdown.

Myth: *We should leave work on a high, while we're still enjoying work.*
Fact: People often endure work to beef up their pension.

Myth: *We should retire comfortably.*
Fact: Only 30 percent of the people surveyed by BlackRock, an investment management company, said they were financially well prepared for retirement; 33 percent said they would likely never be able to retire. Retiring comfortably is no longer a realistic expectation for many people.

Role Models for Retirement

In retirement as in most aspects of life we see how others manage their lives and are either inspired to follow in their footsteps, or avoid doing what they do. Most often it's people close to us who become models for our own lives.

The word retirement had never entered Josée's vocabulary. She admired her mother, who ran a profitable art gallery until shutting it down at 76.

Five hundred days prior to his first retirement, Doug hung a sign above his office door and began to count them down. Many of the staff he'd hired over the years would retire about the same time, but his role model for his real retirement was his wife who was "…retired and enjoying herself with my grandson, and I'm a little jealous. At eleven months, he's the light of our lives. That's the biggest single reason I wish I was elsewhere than at work. I'm looking forward to teaching him how to skate and play hockey." Doug did quit, as planned, but his retirement took the form of going into politics and becoming a cabinet minister.

Molded by Nova Scotian hardiness and her family's industriousness, Linda planned to work until her nineties. She hadn't seen people retire when she was growing up. "Doctors worked until they were ancient. People worked in the stores 'til they were well over 65. I don't think the pulp and paper mill gave pensions. Nobody had pensions. If people didn't work for long years, they died in their sixties. That was the way life was," she said. Her retired friends who played golf and traveled to Florida provided no role models. "I don't play golf nor do I have any desire to, and I don't want to go to Florida." On the occasional day Linda didn't feel like going to work, she would think about her hobby of the moment—carving, working in glass, sewing, or reading a book. Retirement felt like something altogether different. It meant sitting at home or "running out to meetings" and she didn't see herself doing either.

Susan was at the end of her rope and ready to retire from her management job at 59, unable to stay another year for a full pension. Spurring her on were horror stories of people who hung on for one more year and then fell to cancer or a heart attack six months after they retired—she didn't want that to happen to her. She was able to move to a less stressful contract position and retired from government at 60 with a full pension when that position was cut. Susan spent 11 months getting her energy back before she started a four-day-a-week contract position with a not-for-profit organization, which felt do-able for several more years until she and her husband could fully retire together.

Gwen and Don retired with ideas of travelling "because we were at that age" and being available for aging parents. Some of their friends who hadn't been self-employed had retired 15 years earlier. "They were going to retirement classes and we were just getting on our feet. We were years behind." A year after they retired, Don had a cardiac arrest and by-pass operation.

Jan's friends, who had worked in government or companies, some younger than her, were retiring with "lovely" pensions. "A little bit of me is envious, but not really," she said. She imagined they had a degree of financial stability and the ability to do a lot of travelling or whatever they wanted. Her father, who was still writing every day at 92, was more a role model, as were several older women who still worked but wintered in Mexico.

Rhiannon had always thought of retirement as the opportunity to do new things more suited to who she was, and had planned to go back to work after she retired at 65. The first year she did volunteer work and earned a certificate in adult education and a diploma as a career practitioner. When an instructor said, 'Say transition. Don't say retirement,' Rhiannon was inspired to develop and teach her own course, "Re-Wiring: Life after Retirement." Her fully-retired partner didn't understand her need to work; she didn't share his dream of living on a boat. But they agreed to live in Greece for six months and then return to Canada so she could work.

Keith had seen too many people retire from policing and then die, including one guy who died the day after he retired. To him, it was impossible to move from a high-stress occupation to doing nothing. Later, as mayor he saw older people continuing to work, afraid to retire because of what their dollar would bring them;

seniors afraid of losing their houses because they'd lost their job; and others in their eighties who struggled to make ends meet, eventually giving up their homes. He thought they all should be retired and enjoying life, but added, "...maybe they enjoy life working, like me."

Carl's retired friends were miserable, but he was miserable at work, with union staff split by issues and strikes, and animosity between former friends. He no longer felt the rewards or acknowledgement for his efforts. He was being encouraged to apply for management jobs, but those were the first to be slashed in mergers, and his could disappear overnight. Leaving would be painful, but staying was worse.

A Final Word

Some boomers have a traditional retirement squarely in sight and can predict the age they'll retire. Others don't see retirement in their future, and still others are leaving the idea of retirement for later consideration. Two things can be said with certainty: each person will define retirement in their own way, and an increasing number of boomers will include work in their retirement. But what will their work look like? We turn to that in the next chapter.

Activity

Review retirement

Retirement planners say we need to plan what we're going to do with our time and energy after we quit work. Financial planners say we need 75 percent of our take-home income (others say 60 percent) to live comfortably in retirement, or a nestegg of 25 times the amount of money we spend each year. Most of us will not accrue that kind of nest egg.

What's *your* retirement scenario? (These scenarios are modelled after the 1999 AARP study).

1. I'm **troubled** – I can't fully retire because I don't have enough retirement income. I need to be frugal.
2. I'm **traditional** – I like to work and can't afford to retire. Maybe I'll start working for myself.
3. I'm **enthusiastic** -- I have a good pension, and I'm looking forward to doing all the things retirees do.
4. I'll **struggle** – I've never been able to save for retirement and I'll need to work.
5. I'm **self-reliant**. I have some money for retirement, but I'll work at least part-time because it's interesting.

Do you have a different scenario? What does it look like?

Are you putting off the things you really want to do until retirement?

Do you look forward to retirement?

What are your dreams for retirement?

What might push / prompt / permit you to retire? For example, age? Sufficient savings? Health issues? Competing interests? Other?

Seven

Working for the Good Life

It is your work in life that is the ultimate seduction.

— Pablo Picasso

What is it about work that makes it necessary to some and a necessary evil to others? Why do people do the particular work they do? The answers lie in how each of us is wired, in our innate preferences and talents, and in our life experiences.

We've heard the saying "No one on their death bed ever said, 'I didn't work long enough in my life'" so often, it seems to be true. But it's not true for everyone, especially not for those who find great meaning or joy in work, or who still have things to accomplish. There are those who cannot not work, for whom not being engaged in work is unthinkable. There are those who began working later in life who are compensating for career interruptus, those who are workaholics, and those who can't think of anything else to do with their time.

We're challenged to find work that satisfies us. Whether we took into account our own unique abilities and interests when we initially chose our career path, or had any idea about the staggering number of occupations available back then, most of our generation have worked, and we've done it for one reason—to create the good life.

Although we know that work is necessary to achieve the good life, we may be hard-pressed to explain exactly how work does it. As early as Aristotle, in the fourth century B.C., philosophers have weighed in on how to achieve the good life. The new field of positive psychology, which studies the conditions that help us to flourish and attain happiness, offers helpful answers to the questions.

Three Ways to the Good Life

We experience the good life at three levels, said Martin Seligman, the psychologist credited with founding positive psychology. The levels are the life of pleasure, the life of engagement, and the life of meaning. Work is central to all three, giving us pleasure, satisfaction and happiness, three subtly different emotional states.

The life of pleasure is the take-time-to-smell-the-roses level in which we experience objects and activities that deliver immediate albeit brief pleasure. Each of us has preferences for what we find pleasurable. A brief list includes finding enjoyment in different kinds of food, art, or music—making or consuming it, driving cars, taking vacations and traveling, nature, star gazing. We need a variety of pleasurable activities and to experience them frequently throughout the day. If we're savvy, we learn to prolong and savour each moment. We can experience moments of pleasure at work, but what work does well is help us afford pleasurable experiences.

A life of engagement, of being fully involved in an activity—work, play, family life—also leads to the good life. At this level, we experience "flow," says Mihaly Csikszentmihalyi, the psychologist who developed flow theory. Flow is the mental, emotional and physical state we're in when we're so engrossed in what we're doing that we're oblivious to what's going on around us and are unaware of what we're feeling. When we stop doing that all-absorbing activity—gardening, carpentry, counselling, tending animals, cooking, arguing law, fishing, designing bridges, writing computer programs or novels, playing a musical instrument, teaching—the list is endless and individual—we marvel that time has passed, and we feel enveloped by satisfaction. For the good life at this level we need to know our strengths, develop them, and use them regularly. Some people make flow activities their livelihood, but many work to keep body and soul together, endure their jobs, and wait for weekends and holidays to engage in hobbies and activities.

We don't become happy by pursuing happiness directly. To be happy, to experience the good life at the third level, we need to pursue a life of meaning, says Seligman. Happiness is the by-product of engaging in a personally meaningful, goal-directed activity in which we experience flow. Using our highest strengths in the service of something larger than ourselves, perhaps an altruistic cause, leads to sustained happiness. Any sort of work can bring us happiness if it's absorbing, personally meaningful and done for the good of something beyond ourselves.

All three levels are necessary for the good life, but pleasure doesn't make us feel satisfied or happy. To be satisfied, we need to be engaged. To be happy, we need to pursue meaning. The more absorbed and challenged we are, the more likely we are to be happy.

Seligman turned 74 in 2016, still directing the Positive Psychology Center at the University of Pennsylvania, and accepting new graduate students. Csikszentmihalyi, 82 in 2016, co-directs the Quality of Life Research Center at Claremont Graduate University. Each pursues his mission to understand the roots of happiness, well-being and flow.

Work for Satisfaction

Find happiness at work or you will not be happy.

– Christopher Columbus (attrib.)

Whether our strengths and talents are physical, intellectual, social, or spiritual, they're meant to be employed, enjoyed, strengthened and expanded. Doing what we were born to do and do naturally, even without the required education or being paid, matters over the course of our lives. The value of our strengths lies primarily in how we feel about ourselves when we use them, not how much we're remunerated for them nor how much society values them.

In the overall scheme of life it's important to enjoy our work. However, if our work isn't a source of happiness—it can't lead to happiness all the time for everyone—we may feel happy simply because we have a job, or happy about part of the job, or happy about the things outside of work that it provides us.

Continuing in our profession or engaging in work that serves as a bridge to retirement may help us enjoy better physical and mental health, and experience fewer major diseases and functional limitations compared to those who retire fully, say researchers who study the effects of work on older people. That is especially true if our work suits our strengths and fits with our other priorities. But it's not true if we suffer from poor health, if our work doesn't suit us, or if we don't want to work. A surprising number of older people who are still working rate being very satisfied with their lives, while only a small percentage of older working people are very dissatisfied with their lives. The older we get, the more satisfied we are with our lives if we are working, up to the age of 75. There's no evidence that satisfaction decreases after age 75, since researchers apparently haven't studied the effects of employment on workers older than that.

Work contributes to a sense of well-being in several ways. Most important are the social network and sense of accomplishment it provides. Quitting work, with its loss of daily social contact, often leads to a diminished sense of well-being, although escaping a stressful work environment can alleviate the cumulative effects of stress. Earning extra money to spend on non-essentials, rather than the actual amount we earn, can help us feel more satisfied with our lives. Finally, we may feel happy as a result of contributing to something meaningful.

Linda summed up in a few words what work gave her. "Every day I work at the vet's, I come home feeling really satisfied with my day. They're a great bunch of people, and it's a great job. Nobody watches over me. I go and I work until I have done what I need to get done."

Work for Engagement and Purpose

We change and grow throughout our lives by facing and overcoming the challenges at work and non-work activities, and through the push and pull of family life and close relationships. We pursue growth by leaving jobs that no longer challenge us or ones that challenge too much. Turning 60 or 65 doesn't mean that work-related growth ends or should end. For many, it's time to explore and develop new work-related talents with commitment and intention.

As we age, our motives to work change. Early on, a job gave us independence—a car, our first apartment, and money to pay off student loans. It also helped us get established in a career and develop a professional identity. Later, work supported a family and bought a home. In our sixties and beyond, work may continue to provide basic support, but it can also answer an age-old question once more: what shall I do with my life? We want a sense of purpose and to be engaged in something that gives meaning. We feel the urge to align our efforts with our strengths and values, in some cases, strengths we are only just discovering.

We're told that if we define our purpose—the drive to express our unique nature—and do work that capitalizes on our unique strengths and talents, we're more apt to feel satisfaction and happiness.

Purpose is a fuzzy concept, so this explanation may help. We see purpose manifested in people whose work doesn't feel like work to them, when it gives meaning, satisfaction and perhaps connection to others. Ideally, the decisions about choice of career and jobs we've made throughout our life have been influenced by our sense of purpose. Hopefully, too, purpose has been behind the specific skills and abilities we've developed throughout our career. That is, we've combined the need to support ourselves with our need for meaning. For most people, it's through action, through growing within jobs and leaving them to name their purpose or calling, and to say, "This is what my life is about."

Mary answered the question, "What does work give you?" by saying "I would have had a different answer a few years ago, but now, what keeps me working is I love to write. I can't not write. If I went blind, I'd still write." Mary had always got a kick out of seeing her finished work and pleasure from people reading what she had written. "I did that! It's mine," she'd say, as she held that real thing in her hands. She planned to let her last contract go so she could write novels full-time, after she began to earn a reasonable amount from doing so. It was work that absorbed her in which she would keep learning.

The experiences we gain over our lifetime, in turn, shape our inherent nature. We can express purpose in more ways than one, and purpose may not change at this stage of life so much as take on new expression.

In the course she took, Transforming Your Working and Living, *Cora proclaimed for the first time that her purpose was to write, even though she had always loved to write. Having retired at 55 from teaching high school English and specializing in remedial reading, by 65 she had written one book, had begun writing a blog for a grocery store's website, edited a book and several students' theses, and operated a small business in which she taught people in business to write so their messages in emails and reports were accurately conveyed.*

Clarifying purpose is a process. Deciding what you want to do—not just can do or have done—takes time, although spending a lot of time just thinking about it isn't productive; besides it can tie you in knots. It helps to reflect on experiences and even long-past dreams, to sift through what you like, what gets you excited, even what you don't want to do, but purpose is found, or discovered if you like, through doing. When you find clarity it may not be profound so much as ring true. If clarity suggests bold, new action, your resolve to pursue a life of purpose might wobble, since it's easy to be seduced by life as you know it, by a regular income, pensions and hard-won professional identity. It's easy, too, to be put off by the belief that you're too old to do something new. From time to time ask yourself, What do I need to be doing? to help maintain resolve as you steer a new course.

Having a sense of purpose and having fun, making money, and most importantly, making a difference all lured Doug to work. When he worked at Yukon College, a highlight was watching young people succeed. "You can have an amazing influence on people, if you try." Yukon's Minister of Health and Social Services when we talked, Doug enjoyed what he was doing, but there were things he'd rather be doing. "I can see myself ending my political career at

67 or 68. I can't see going beyond that. It would take something extra special to get me to come back after that, something I really wanted to do. My wife will be impatient for me to retire by then. I hope to have a number of projects completed before I leave," he said. He spoke about a wellness policy for social inclusion and poverty reduction underway in the Territory: *"One of the things that would make me come back to political office would be if the things I think should be in place for not only kids and adults but seniors as well, weren't in place."*

Two knee replacements and a divorce when she was 57 turned Jan's life upside down. *"It made me think furiously about who I was. I realized consciously, unconsciously, that it was all bound up for me, that I really liked my work and would like to keep on to some degree probably the rest of my life."*

Owning and operating The Violin Doctor was a way for William to meet people and to listen to their stories. He had enjoyed teaching, and being the Doctor and renting violins to young learners helped him to continue working with young people. He wanted to help them take their initial interest in violin to a level beyond playing a few tunes, and hoped they would absorb lessons about discipline, learn to manage time, stand on a stage with confidence, and feel joy.

Pairing Passion and Riches

"Follow your passion and the money will follow" the saying goes, implying untold riches will come your way if you do. Countless books expound this idea—making their authors rich. But where is the book by the guy who followed his passion and broke even or worse, went in the hole, and then fought his way out, or the gal who followed her passion and lives a perfectly ordinary life?

Passion is an equally fuzzy concept. Less than 20 percent of any age group actually know their passion and how to fulfill it, says Bill Burnett, who teaches students the principles of designing their life at Stanford University.

Still, many of the boomers I talked to were following their passion, some turning their passions into viable businesses.

"What else would I do?" said Stephen when I asked why he'd gone back to work. At 56 after a long career in Canada's food industry, he had retired with no plans for what he'd do next. Six months later, boredom, as well as the intense satisfaction he always felt when solving problems businesses faced, drove him to start a consulting practice doing what he loved. That ended after six months when he accepted a job offer from a food company in Quebec to bring to fruition the strategy he'd developed to expand their operations.

Jim, who grew up in post-war England, developed a passion for collectibles alongside his father, who was an expert in war medals. As a child, Jim had roamed the countryside with friends, unearthing antiquities and war debris. As an adult, he scouted garage sales and charity-run second-hand shops, spotting treasures to sell on eBay, Kijiji and in local antique shops. It was a satisfying and profitable part-time business—operating costs were low and most months it gave him half his income. "Someday I'm going to find the picture of an ugly flower that'll bring me a million dollars...I don't think it's going to happen. Certainly I find little things that bring me two or three hundred dollars on a minimal investment."

Elle paired her fascination with the history of northwestern Ontario with her love of writing. She launched her own publishing company to publish the niche-market books she predicted big publishers wouldn't publish.

Several people wouldn't turn their passion into a business, because they judged that the economic climate couldn't support it or they didn't have qualities to be self-employed.

Linda had turned one of her employer's receipts-in-a-shoebox set-up into an organized business. It was the kind of service she would love to provide to more small businesses. But although people in her neck of Nova Scotia might well need their bookkeeping organized, and she would like to be the one to do it, she wasn't convinced they would pay for it, so it remained an idea on the shelf.

Designing houses was work David could do forever. It could also be a successful one-man business, but he wasn't the guy to do it, he said, since he lacked the qualities necessary to get a business off the ground. Having migrated to the west coast, he still designed houses part-time for his employer in Ontario, while they waited for the luxury home market to recover.

Some exercise their passion in a job or politics.

After decades as a police officer, Keith, about to become a grandfather, veered into politics. Shunning advice, Keith set his sights on the top city job. His leap landed him squarely in the mayor's chair, where he was passionate about the responsibility and possibilities. He admitted he tends to be a workaholic and was happily using that quality to lead the city from being "stuck-in-neutral" to one with a growing population and more industry, and in the long run, in better shape for his grandchildren. (Workaholism is a buzzword with negative connotations; it's not workaholism when you enjoy your work and derive satisfaction).

It was feeling connected with clients as they learned to manage their addictions that made work worthwhile to Gene. During his half-hour commute to work each morning, he often wondered how long he was going to keep doing it, but on his way home at night he often thought, "I know why I came to work today."

Beyond Purpose and Money

Besides the usual reasons, we enjoy other advantages of work. Health benefits and perks are two.

Jim was pretty drained at the end of his 12-hour days at the casino and didn't feel like putting together more than a peanut butter sandwich and cup of tea, so he enjoyed the low-cost, full-course meals. "They can keep me there 'til I'm 75," he quipped. PJ didn't mind staying around at work a little longer because she knew that a lot of corporate knowledge would disappear when boomers retire.

A Final Word

Finances and purpose are the two main drivers in our decision to work to have the good life, but people also talked about the satisfaction they felt doing what they loved. That in itself is a form of wealth.

However, in our sixties, we encounter a number of issues in getting a job. We'll read about them next.

Activity

Your work and the good life

Pleasure
Is work an environment where you enjoy moments of pleasure?

Satisfaction
Do you "get lost" in your work?

On a scale of 1 to 10 how important is it to you to be engrossed in your work?

Meaning
At the end of the day do you say, "I know why I went to work today?"

At day's end do you feel that what you did mattered?

Purpose and Passion
Now, in this later stage of your career, how important is it to you to feel passionate about your work?

Eight

Older Workers at Work

The umpteenth time I was asked "How much longer are you going to work?" I searched for inspiration from "the world's oldest employee." Curiously, I found more men than women.

- "Buster" Martin of London, England took the prize, although the facts of his life are disputed. At 99, after two years of boredom in retirement, Martin went back to work three days a week cleaning vans. At 101 he was training to run the London marathon, having just completed a half-marathon.
- Arthur Winston of Los Angeles, named 'Employee of the Century' by Bill Clinton in 1996, was acknowledged for his work ethic and dedication. Winston retired at 100 after 76 years with city transit agencies, and died in 2006, one month after he retired.
- Patsy Maida celebrated his 90th birthday in 2010 with fellow employees at Hartford, Connecticut's D&D Supermarket, where he started work in the meat department in the1960s.
- Loraine Maurer, 94, celebrated 44 years of service at McDonald's in Evansville, Indiana, with customers, fellow employees and the fast food chain. She has no plans to retire.

Admittedly, working into our nineties won't be attractive to many, but deciding how long you'll work requires some thought. We've read about the things that motivate us to work, but our health, our competing interests and the changing environment of work, among other things, influence how long we'll work and the way we'll work.

How Much Longer Will You Work?

I asked people to predict the age at which they would quit work. Some said their health would dictate when they'd quit. Others said the time to retire would be when, and if, they felt ready to quit. A few either had no intention of quitting or didn't foresee the possibility of ever quitting work.

- *Norm would quit work when he's 69 or 70.*
- *Josée, when she's 70.*
- *Gene, when he's 70.*
- *Ole would quit full-time work when he's 68 and planned to work part-time after that.*
- *Ruth would work as long as it felt like a good thing to do.*
- *Keith wanted to do two four-year terms as mayor (so it depended on voters), taking him to 66. In the future he'd figure out what follows, but he wasn't thinking about retiring.*
- *Stephen, 56, didn't have an answer. Instead, he asked himself, "How am I going to spend the next 10, 15 years, and is it going to be working?"*
- *"I see ending my political career at 67 or 68," said Doug at 62. "It would take something extra special to get me to come back after that, unless I had something I really wanted to do."*
- *At 62, PJ said she'd work 'til she's 71. "I'm young enough to still have a lot to give."*

"If I wasn't working I don't know what I'd do with myself," PJ said. Pressed to say the age at which she'd quit, she picked 71, nine years older than women's average retirement age today. In 1996 in her mid-forties, she took an early retirement package then did "all sorts of work" for 10 years. When we talked PJ worked in a cubicle with a view, among people who seemed to like going to work. She liked the responsibility she carried and felt satisfied at day's end, having completed piles of transactions that ensured provincial and territorial health care systems paid for their citizens' care while travelling in other provinces and territories.

I asked Linda, then 64, if she'd still be working in ten years. "I have no doubt I'll want to work as much as I am now. As long as I'm as healthy as I am now, I'd like to work at least four days a week, perhaps five. As long as I'm healthy, I wouldn't change it if I was 94."

After 20 years with the railroad, David was laid off in his forties, ending a career he expected to last 'til retirement. He took a buy-out but didn't get the pension. He looked for work for two years before he landed a contract designing luxury houses his employer constructed around the world. Ten years later, the 2008 economic melt-down put him out of work once more. He looked for work for another two years before he found work again. David concluded he'd work until three days before his funeral.

We're apt to be told we're depriving younger people of a job, but that's not true. Although some occupations beg for workers due to skills shortages in Canada, young people and older people don't often compete for the same jobs. PJ didn't think she was taking anyone's job; she had been trained to do hers by someone about her own age.

Using Tools to Predict How Long to Work

We can't see into the future, but there are tools we can consult that calculate how long we can expect to work.

I fed my personal data into the electronic wizard at www.brownecon.com. It spit out that I'd work to 70.7 and live to 86, based on my sex, level of education and age—female, university grad and 66 at the time. When I entered high-school educated male, the program said I'd work until I was 76.2 and live to 82.6. The program failed to ask about my psychological attachment to work or the amount of money I'd saved, two factors that affect my decision.

More useful is the **Working Life Expectancy Scale** (WLE) developed by researchers in Finland, which doesn't provide you with an age. It does, however, pose thoughtful questions. Assuming that disability, morbidity (the rate at which people of a particular population become sick or diseased) and mortality (the average age of death of a particular population) stay at their current level, the Scale asks you to estimate six factors.

- an estimate of your present ability to work compared with your lifetime best,
- your perceived ability to work in relation to the physical and mental demands of your work,
- the number of diagnosed diseases you have,
- an estimate of how impaired you are for work as a result of absence(s) from work due to disease and sickness during the past year,
- your prediction of your ability to work two years into the future, and
- your psychological resources, that is, your ability to psychologically manage the demands of work.

You get a rating of your working life expectancy, from excellent to good, fair or poor. Improving one or two factors—obviously not all factors can be changed—will increase your overall ability to work. For instance, you can decrease a job's demands and increase your psychological resources, which include such things as knowledge of self, personal management skills, continuing to learn and exploring work, the skills to manage transitions, and striking a balance between work and non-work. However, if you simply believe that being of an older age hinders your ability to work, you could skew your estimate of your present ability to work.

Activity

What's your working life expectancy?

Answer the six factors above to get an estimate of how long you'll work.

Finally, when you think of how long you'll work, you needn't think in terms of the number of years. It's an arbitrary concept that invites us to control the future rather than let it unfold as it will. That doesn't say we shouldn't plan for the future; rather we can make decisions when it seems like the right time to do so. Now, more than earlier in our lives, work needs to fit our changing physical and lifestyle needs, and we need to adjust to the changing landscape of the technological age.

PHYSICAL CHANGES

It's commonly believed that work performance decreases with age; however, there is no consistently demonstrated relationship between the two. Still, we look for ways to reduce physical harm to our bodies at work and away from work.

We're not as flexible and strong as we were. Our vision and hearing have begun to deteriorate. Our mobility and balance are reduced. Our reaction times are slower. We're more apt to suffer from eye strain, hearing difficulties and repetitive motion injuries and accidents.

Modifications in work environments, such as increased lighting and ergonomic work stations, help to ensure our safety and health, and even seduce us to keep working. To work at computers we need more light, glare-less monitors set at an altered viewing distance, and mid-range prescriptions for glasses. In manufacturing settings, it's better if less strength is needed, and stretching and bending are reduced. Ford Motor's "Happy Seat," is an example; it's a mobile swivel chair that provides better lumbar support and reduces back strain, built right into the assembly line.

Adapting the work environment to suit older workers will come slowly. After teaching firearms at the Ontario Policy Academy in eastern Ontario for three years, Keith returned to Thunder Bay, expecting to find a suitable position in its police service. "It's like they put an older person in crappy jobs and on shifts to get rid of you and, at 57, 58, you don't want to be scrapping with drunks," he said. When he found nothing suitable, Keith retired and entered politics.

Generally, we're less able to do shift work.

Norm was driving bus at a Fort McMurray work-site. He'd found that a split shift could relieve the stress of a long day. He appreciated that his workday had a beginning and an end, and didn't go on for days and days, like his previous work had as a long-distance trucker. "I could've stayed trucking a while longer, but I needed more challenge. This job isn't more challenging, but I have time in the middle of the day that's mine, and I'm home more, solidly home. I can be in this job for a long time. But there'll come a time when I physically can't do it, when I slowly start to fade away."

Gene had counselled on the front-line of addictions treatment for 26 years, and felt too old to counsel in an intense environment such as the residential treatment centre, where he once worked. He was often encouraged to become a supervisor, but wasn't interested in administration and meetings, either.

Two couples, Gwen and Don and Ole and Karen, retired from their businesses when they felt the size of the workload, the long days and weeks with no breaks, and the intensity of the work were becoming too much. Ole and Karen sold their business and moved to a smaller community to do slower-paced work, while Don and Gwen retired, to help out occasionally in their son's and daughter's businesses.

BALANCING WORK AND FAMILY

We raised our kids, juggling their needs with our job. Finally, we have time to give to our families and don't have to choose between their needs and work. But it's not our own kids' needs we're meeting now, it's the needs of our grandchildren. And, we're transforming the role of grandparent.

Even though Keith's first grandchild wasn't yet born, he was looking forward to caring for that child, much like his parents had looked after his children. He made lunch appointments with his son—though he thought making an appointment with your kid is pathetic—and he had a standing once-a-week date with his partner, allowing work to be a priority. But when he becomes a grandfather, he anticipated that work would clash with his new role.

Doug was the perfect sandwich-generation guy. His mother, who was visually impaired, lived with him and his wife, and often their one-year old grandson stayed with them. Doug and his wife had retired within a month of each other. Six months after retiring, Doug entered Yukon's politics, although he envied aspects of his wife's retirement. "She's enjoying the heck out of herself with my grandson, and I'm a little jealous. A grandson is much different than having kids at a younger age. He's the light of our lives. I've always said that as soon as he started walking, he was getting on skates, because I love to play hockey, still, and I want him to be another Wayne Gretzky. But I'll make time for him next year during the day, and he'll be skating and all those other things I know little boys should do, and little girls," he said.

Most mornings Doug and his wife would go for a run before he went to work. "Physically it's not taxing, those 10-hour work days when the legislature is in session," he said. "But mentally it is, because I sit here at one o'clock on Tuesday and Thursday afternoons thinking, I should be out playing in the 55-and-over league and I can't. Those kinds of things bother me, but I love politics, so I'll put up with this for a while." Before he retired, for years Doug was able to map out free time during the day to leave work two afternoons a week to play hockey, and make up the time later. After serving as a cabinet minister, he was thinking about going back to sit as an MLA so he could have more day-time freedom, to be involved in caring for his grandchildren.

When Mary's daughter was seven, she had booked herself into Mary's day planner. With that wake-up call, Mary tried to negotiate terms with her business partner so she could work from home more and to re-schedule 7:30 am meetings to after she took her daughter to school. Her partner's initial answer had been an offer to buy her out. The incident stuck in Mary's memory: she was going to take time off work with no qualms, to be with her daughter when her soon-to-be-born granddaughter arrived and to be available from then on when she was needed.

Norm's work in Fort McMurray allowed him to be home one week in three. This gave him time to be with his wife, enjoy dinner parties, take on building projects, and ski with his granddaughters, a new activity he was fond of.

As mayor of Whitehorse, Bev often put in more than full-time hours. Her long hours meant she was seldom available to family and friends, who, she believed, understood how important it was for her to do what she was doing. After serving her term as mayor, she would continue to work, but she hoped to have more free time.

CARING FOR PARENTS

Canada's policies on caregiving are based on the assumption that it's the family's responsibility to care for its elder members, and that the family wants to and is able to do the caretaking. The 2012 General Social Survey found that 28 percent of those aged 15 and over had provided care for a family member in the preceding year. Nearly one-quarter of those were aged 45 to 54 (the number increased by 20 percent since the 2007 survey) and one-fifth were 55 to 64. Taking all caregivers into account, most caregivers spent less than 10 hours a week providing care, but one in 10 provided care for more than 30 hours a week. Fifty-four percent of caregivers were women, and they spent more time than men in caregiving tasks.

More than 80 percent of people (in the 2007 Social Survey) who had simultaneous responsibilities for raising their own children and caring for people 65 years and older were working. The demands of three competing duties—a job, caregiving, and one's own family—force a person to change their work schedule (and their social activities). Loss of income has not been calculated when caregivers, mostly women, take time off during the day, take leaves, refuse overtime and promotions, and lose benefits when they cut back hours to care for a loved one. Caregiving also pushes both men and women to retire earlier than those who don't provide care. A Catch-22 is that care-giving often comes with extra expenses, making work more important. Regardless, we want flexible hours at work so we can pony up to our family responsibilities.

When my mother was diagnosed with cancer, I was working part-time and able to make the 1000-kilometre round-trip to drive her to medical appointments and spend time with her. Years later I'm still thankful for that opportunity.

Rick was able to care for his wife and do his job, staying late at work if he had to, to make up the time he'd take off during the day to take his wife to medical appointments or respond to her emergencies.

While Bunny worked part-time, on her days off she often found herself chauffeuring her mother and aunt to medical appointments and such. When she went back to work full-time, Bunny found she could still manage a full-time job and fit in necessary appointments by declaring to her supervisor that she wouldn't be in.

Caregiving parents was more difficult for Don and Gwen while they worked. Had anyone in their families needed their help during tax season, they would have felt torn between their obligation to work and their desperation to care for parents. It's a choice they never had to make, but they retired in part to be available to care for parents who lived two provinces away.

Compassion care leave allows family members to take time off work, without pay, to care for gravely ill family members, a provision available across Canada through the Employment Insurance Act. The person taking leave must be the primary caregiver, and is eligible for up to 6 weeks of E.I. benefits, with a two-week waiting period.

What Suits Us Now

PORTFOLIO CAREERS
There's a troubling trend: traditional permanent, jobs-for-life continue to disappear, and employers hire freelancers and short-term employees to do work formerly done by full-time employees. Increasingly people are forced to rely on a series of casual, contract and temporary jobs, at times holding more than one type of short-term job at a time. A year after the 2008 economic downturn, one in eight workers in Canada held some form of temporary employment, according to Statistics Canada.

The career industry calls careers built on such work portfolio careers. This non-traditional approach to employment suits many boomers to a T, since it combines well the ability to earn an income, take care of family and enjoy more leisure time.

Sally stitched together three parts in her portfolio career. The major part was contracting with individuals and institutions for her editorial and writing services. At times the pressure to earn each month's income felt burdensome, but Sally saw no alternatives, since the strict regimen of a job and a boss watching over her comings and goings would feel impossible. She didn't feel able to turn contracts down, at times working seven days a week to juggle the load. In the summer she topped up her income by working as a tour guide and hosting her own ghost tours in Victoria. "The editing projects are always interesting and varied, and my lifestyle and activities are varied too, so that suits me fine. I'm always learning," she said.

Carl and Arlene usually had at least three things on the go all the time. They worked together in their landscaping and gardening business. He drove school bus, did renovations and data wiring, while she worked seasonally in a greenhouse and did some book-keeping. One year after his retirement they were feeling their way, but their combination fit, since Carl liked to be busy. A surprise was that money was easily made and that they had a higher income than when he had a full-time job.

Ruth's series of part-time jobs had served her need to structure part of her week, have social contact, and observe and learn about people's behaviour. Jobs came to her, and she had no difficulty quitting them when they no longer suited her.

Volunteer work

Retirement coaches urge us to find something to immerse ourselves in, suggesting that volunteer work can bring satisfaction and meaning. Not everyone agreed.

Rick couldn't just do volunteer work, since volunteering could be costly with various expenses such as gasoline.

William, The Violin Doctor, was firmly against volunteerism; he didn't see responsibility and challenge in volunteer positions. Rhiannon, who had volunteered after she retired, saw volunteers as peripheral, people with no real power.

Terri, a university professor, was a bit ticked when she was asked to fold paper napkins into flowers at the professional conference she had volunteered to help with.

On the other hand PJ's volunteer work aligned with her interests and her commitment to her community's emergency response plan. A ham radio operator, PJ was one of a team that did a nightly radio check-in, which she convened every Friday. The team met monthly, while her sub-group met weekly, the meetings creating part of her social life. In the event of an emergency, she could be part of the emergency measures response. She also edited her service club's newsletter, which put her in contact with people from the Yukon, Alaska and Russia. Though important, these wouldn't be enough for her in retirement.

Volunteer jobs are often stepping stones to paid work, as today's young job seeker knows. It applies to boomers as well. Volunteering can lead to a job even when we haven't volunteered to get experience.

Elle wasn't intentionally building a career as she wrote and coordinated public service announcements and press releases at local, provincial and eventually national levels as a volunteer for a not-for-profit health organization. Over the years she developed increasingly specialized skills, and in one media campaign she even worked with Michael J. Fox. Only when a friend, by chance, told her she should get paid for her work, did Elle see the possibility. Soon after, at 48, she landed her first paid writing job. Years later she didn't see going back to producing her work for free. "I'm at a point where I'm paid for it. It makes a good living for me."

Laura, a professor of nursing in Spain, came to Canada with her husband when she was 53. She couldn't speak English so couldn't be registered by the provincial body. She went to language classes in the morning and stocked shelves in a big-box building supplies store in the afternoon. To practice English more, she began to volunteer at an immigrant-serving health agency, with the long-term goal of working her way up to use her experience.

Commute to work

Government and industry say we have a shortage of skilled workers. In some occupations shortages are regional. There's work in the north, for instance. The challenge is to convince workers to move for a job.

The older we get, the more apt we are to stay put in our own province. If we move at all, we move to retire rather than to work. For some, long-distance commuting is the answer.

Up until the drop in oil prices in 2014, workers flocked to the west to find work in the oil sands and oil sands-driven economy. Many of them commuted, eliminating the need to pull up roots. Each week dozens of red-eye and charter flights shuttled commuters back and forth across Canada. How do people manage to live in one region and work in another?

Norm lived two of every three weeks in a Fort McMurray camp with 84 other drivers who shuttled workers between the work-site and their camp home-away-from-home.

On the east coast, the "Newfoundland ladies," as they came to be called, supported their families after the Newfoundland fishing industry tanked, by working in Nova Scotia, a CBC television documentary said. One-by-one they traveled by bus and ferry to work for two weeks as live-in personal aides, caring for physically dependent people in their homes, then returned home for two weeks to carry on their normal life.

Canadians also commute for seasonal and locum work. *Helen, 64, spent four months—tax season—each winter in Calgary, working for a friend, an accountant. Graham, a 60-year old social worker, headed to Nunavut several times a year to do relief work when he wasn't working in a hospital.*

After she retires at 65, Julie hoped to take her passion for preventative health care to northern Canada, alternating working six to eight weeks with populations struggling with addictions and suicide, with six to eight weeks at home.

After they sold their trucking business and home, Karen and Ole divided their time between the small, remote community on BC's central coast, where they worked, and their patio home on Vancouver Island. When Karen found winters long on the coast or when work was scarce, they headed south on the ferry and returned in the spring, where a favourite past-time was fishing for prawn and crab in the rich coastal waters.

Boomer Women's History at Work

The ups and downs of women's employment history say much about why many older women are still working. Boomer women came of age during the second wave of feminism that began in the early sixties. In 1971, only 54 percent of Canadian boomer women, then aged 16 to 25, were employed, and the wage difference between women and men was greater than today. Today, women can look back at their years of employment with nostalgia, horror, sadness, hilarity, and remorse; they might also view the changes in the work world in the last 50 years with gratitude.

A few months after the 2008 economic collapse, I watched a man on the news lament that his wife had begun to work; she was babysitting their grandchildren. He'd been laid off after yet another plant had closed in southwestern Ontario, and his employment prospects weren't good. Some forty years earlier, along with his marriage vows he had pledged she would never have to work, and he'd been able to keep his promise. Now, in his eyes, he had failed.

That wasn't an uncommon promise for young boomers. *Although no man made that promise to me, and I didn't expect one to do so, I took it for granted I'd never "have to" work. Work was a fallback position, my mother advised me, in case I ended up a widow as she had. When I was 24, my short marriage fell apart. My husband's father, intervening on his son's behalf, told me that my having a job and being a career woman (I hadn't thought of myself as one) was the root of our problems. His solution: I should quit and have a baby.*

The stories women told me about their work history struck a chord.

Mary called her career "wild and woolly." It began with a degree in journalism, which landed her a job in the newsroom of a large Canadian daily newspaper. Two weeks after she started work, an editor hit on her. She left and turned to communications and public relations. Still early in her career, a company director told her she didn't need a salary increase that would bring her in line with her male colleagues because she had a husband who made money. Such affronts, which many women have experienced, fueled Mary's drive to succeed. More recently, Mary had become sole bread-winner for her and her husband after he retired, burned out from his work. Used to making good money, she faced an anxious period after her cancer diagnosis, when she couldn't land contracts.

Women of the sixties who stepped off the education path after high school didn't expect they'd get back on. When they entered the workforce they were often told they were taking a job away from men, even when they held the usual roles—nurses, elementary (not high) school teachers, secretaries, and sales and bank clerks. It was education or family at a time when fewer women were encouraged to get a post-secondary education.

After high school, Julie married an older man from her immigrant community, ignoring her dream to become a nurse. Her parents approved, reasoning he would look after her. When her dream resurfaced in her thirties, she couldn't ignore it. She spent a year in high school and three years in nursing school, while shouldering the entire load of housework, her homework, helping the children with their homework and commuting two hours each day. She felt like giving up at times, but she was spurred on by the spectre of spending her life as a waitress, married to a man who threatened to shoot her if she left him.

Parents' or others' paternalistic hands have tried to steer our careers.

Although her father never said it explicitly, PJ believed he would have liked her to take hairdressing. She took electronics technology instead.

When Cora applied for a vice-principal position after teaching one year with a temporary certificate, the principal told her he'd given the job to a man because he had a family to look after. Meanwhile, her recently widowed father, in cahoots with the school superintendent, finagled a job for her in her hometown so she could live at home and look after her small siblings. But Cora had applied to a public school board further away. Although she didn't recall ticking the religion box, the superintendent passed her application to the Catholic board, which offered her a job. (Religion used to be a standard question on job application forms).

Women who are single parents and the family bread winner have often needed to decide whether they can take a job or not.

Sally had a varied work history and had lived in three countries by the time she came to Canada at 33. Passionate about the preservation of historical landmark buildings, she earned a master's degree in urban planning in her early fifties. During the downsizing deluge in the early 1990s, her education was no ticket to a job. To gain experience she might have found work "in the boonies", but she didn't want to move her children nor leave them behind in the city.

Susan was the family's main earner for most of her marriage, supporting her family of four while her husband operated a karate school. Her two maternity leaves were short—four months—because they could live on EI only so long. In her early sixties, in the pressure cooker role of writing government policy, Susan grew increasingly discouraged, but being the family breadwinner, she felt unable to quit.

Looking for Work

If the last time you applied for a job, you banged out your resume on an electric typewriter or filled out an application form by hand, you can be saluted for having held the same job for decades or for having had a benevolent source of income.

Finding a new job is daunting. If there's a bright spot, it's that we Canadians fare better than job seekers in other countries. Anne-Marie Guillemard, a French sociologist, quoted in a 2011 Time Magazine article, says that it's impossible for anyone over 55 in France to find employment, a country with an "early exit culture" as well as the lowest average retirement age in the European Union, 59.4 in 2010.

"I thought I was an old guy for the workplace twelve years ago, when I was forty-three, beyond the middle of my working life," said David. "I said that to a buddy and he laughed, because he had just changed jobs. Now I'm that much older. I've been laid off twice, so it's really difficult to get your head around that. A statistic in the job-finding club I went to was: anybody starting out in the workforce today can expect to be laid off or lose their job seven times in their working life. Finding a job once is hard enough. Finding one seven times...I can't fathom."

We don't expect to have to take a stepping-stone job to get a foot-hold—perhaps only a toe-hold—to enter a new sector.

Lynne had to, when she set about making her debut into public school teaching. Her first year looking for work in BC's lower mainland "beat the snot" out of her, as she vied with dozens of applicants for as little as quarter-time positions. Although qualified in her subject area, she couldn't compete against teachers who had union seniority but sometimes little content knowledge. "You gotta wait for somebody to get sick or die to get their job," she said, struggling to be grateful that she was getting some part-time substitute work.

It's a long process, and we learn much along the way, since the advertisement of jobs, recruitment methods, vetting and hiring of candidates is always changing. ThirdQuarter, a national non-profit organization serving job seekers aged 45 and over suggests that it takes an average of one month of searching for every $10,000 expected in salary to secure a job—five months for a $50,000 job, 10 months for $100,000. (The ThirdQuarter website boasts a job board, a place to post your profile, emails offering advice about positioning yourself in the job search, job seekers' cafes in various parts of the country).

What Employers Want

Employers hope the candidate who walks into the interview possesses good communication, interpersonal and teamwork skills, and most of the necessary qualifications.

They want older workers to have up-to-date qualifications, a concentration of experience in the designated field although we shouldn't be overspecialized, and technological skills. Employers, who hired over 50-workers, believed we are more productive and require less supervision and training, said a survey conducted by ThirdQuarter. But, employers fear we haven't kept our credentials up-to-date and can't handle a technological environment, that we won't pursue further job training, and we'll get sick, although they believe we won't leave for another employer.

At best, employers' preconceptions of older workers are mixed, but negative preconceptions often blind an employer to qualified, older candidates. It's up to us to dispel any preconceptions right in the interview, by proving that they don't apply to us.

Our challenge is to get an interview. Psychologist Nancy Irwin says age isn't a factor. Older workers should never apologize for their age, especially at an interview. Mentioning it, even obliquely or as a joke can "put off the interview." Recruiters want to know about our experience, skills and wisdom, and whether we'll fit into their organization.

Bunny flaunted that wisdom when she was asked at an interview what she'd bring to the company. "I started thinking, well, I'm old so I have years of experience working with numbers and figures and balancing things. I was being a smart ass and said, 'I guess you can tell by the colour of my hair I won't be going on maternity leave any time soon.' [The interviewer] kind of thought about that and then said, 'Good point, we do get people going on maternity leave.' I had applied on a position for part-time teller and I thought that might be a good thing because I would be reliable. A few days later I got a phone call offering me the job and I jumped at it."

Employers tend to hire older workers for different reasons than they hire younger ones. More often, we're hired to fill a certain position, since employers think we're no longer on a career trajectory and won't bring anything extra to the job, while younger applicants are asked how a job fits with their career plans and how they'll contribute to the organization, in addition to the usual job-specific questions.

We need to decide if we'll be more than a bum-in-chair waiting for retirement, and think about the extras we might bring to a job. Employers want to hear interviewees talk about what they'll bring to the company. They want employees on a learning mission, who can talk about past experience in relation to their future goals, not employees in a holding pattern.

Disappointed after several interviews that brought no job offers, one woman decided that employers seem to want to hire an ethical 32-year old with 20 years of experience.

After 31 years with the same company, Rick's severance package included job transition support: career counselling and help with job search. At 60, he wrote his first ever resume and had his first job interview, and for a year he got short gigs doing payroll and benefits through a temp agency. Then an acquaintance suggested he apply to the government to be a courier driver. After interviewing him, folks in HR decided he might not know the city well enough so they shunted his application into a competition for mail-room sorter. Feeling ticked about that presumption, Rick convinced HR he was the man for the job.

Career Guidance

Who knew we would need career guidance in our sixties? Career guidance is beneficial when it's geared to our needs. A set of principles and programs, called Third Age Guidance (TAG), is designed to help Third Agers make career decisions and search for work.

The ThirdQuarter website offers advice geared to the challenges we experience and even urges us to work with a career coach. Specifically, we need to tailor our resume so it's selected by a company's Applicant Tracking System (ATS), a software program that screens resumes electronically. An ATS matches the keywords and phrases in a job posting to those in a resume (among other things). If there isn't a sufficient match of terms, the program doesn't select the resume for the competition.

Using networks

Our most valuable resource in job searches is our network of friends and acquaintances, present and former colleagues, relatives and neighbours. One or another is bound to know about jobs or contracts and be willing to pass on a lead to us.

Rick's job lead to be a courier driver came through an acquaintance in his condo building who worked in the department.

Always promoting her business in search of the next contract was standard for Sally, who frequently got new contracts from referrals from previous jobs.

Stephen started his consulting business by putting the word out to his network that he was available and had work immediately, however while he was doing a contract, he was too busy to secure the next one so had to let his network know once again that he was available.

Bunny benefited from this type of recognition when she applied to government. Someone spotted her name as her application was being processed in HR and told the boss, "Guess who's back. We gotta get her," landing Bunny a higher-level job and more money.

At times our network fails to deliver.

When Mary approached people in hers, she was greeted cordially but received no referrals.

One woman's previous contract work at a university was no help when she applied for permanent positions. She would get interviews, but nothing more. After she interviewed for an opening in a department she'd previously worked for, HR told the supervisor, who wanted to hire her, to hire a younger applicant. Later she was hired on a three-month contract to clean up some of his work. After another interview she heard through the grapevine that the people doing the hiring had said, 'She'll give us five years, and then she'll retire.'

TECHNO-SAURS COME OF AGE

Let's face it: we aren't very tech savvy. We often hesitate to adapt to ever-changing technology and we learn it slowly. Sixty percent of older boomers used the internet, Statistics Canada found in a 2010 survey. Sixty-one percent of Anglophone seniors owned a cellphone, but only 17 percent owned a smartphone, said a 2014 news story, referencing a report by the Media Technology Monitor.

Older Canadians use the internet to communicate with their social network, typically learning only what is needed for work and is immediately relevant. We need to be pushed to learn.

Sally overcame terrifying learning curves as she switched from paper-and-pencil editing to working on a computer. When Cora began writing material for a grocery store's website, she needed to learn about search engine optimizers (SEOs) to make the company's website more visible. Jim easily adapted to marketing merchandise around the world on-line, using existing websites. But, if we're not going to learn a particular technological skill, then we can buy the service, as Elle did. She paid professionals to lay out a book electronically, reasoning that the time she'd need to learn how to do it was better spent writing.

LinkedIn is an online professional networking website that serves people who want to remain relevant in today's work world. On LinkedIn you create a profile page of yourself to post your skills, professional accomplishments, and education. Prospective employers refer to it to check out the profiles and photos of job candidates, and the groups they belong to. They check Facebook, too, to determine whether applicants are the sort of people who would fit in their organization; they scrutinize the friends and connections in applicants' networks, and the tone of comments and photos they post. Armed with such information they eliminate applicants from the competition.

Today's work world is constantly growing and changing. In order to find work and thrive we need social and professional networks, an online presence, investment in skills development, and updated skills and resources.

Facing Unemployment

The older we are, the longer we've been out of work and the less education we have, the harder it is to get back to work. Older workers, who are unemployed or who work in threatened industries and are at risk of unemployment, need: training with work experience built into it in order to beef up their resumes; help finding work; and a few doors opened for them, such as being marketed to employers, says Human Resources and Skills Development Canada.

Entry-level jobs

Entry level jobs make the world go 'round. Sales associate at a big box store, school bus driver, Tim's coffee jockey, mystery shopper, supermarket food products demonstrator or checkout clerk, call centre associate, data enterer, census or elections worker. Not everyone wants to start at the bottom, but a few of the seasoned workers I talked to found benefits on the bottom rung.

Laura saw her shelf-stocking job as a stepping stone, gaining Canadian experience to put on her resume, and as an impetus to re-establish her career. Ruth's jobs felt more real than a classroom and a pleasant relief. Donald came home energized from the busy, service-oriented atmosphere of a car rental desk, and had moved up to manager. Arlene liked working alongside other women in the greenhouse and got to garden all year 'round. When I was 60 I worked Saturdays in a busy restaurant kitchen, at the most entry level of jobs, kitchen helper. I've always fancied myself a cook, and in the throes of changing careers, I wondered if owning a restaurant could be next. A few months into the job I was asked to expand the deli and take-out part of the business.

If you've worked at higher rungs on the ladder career, you might not want an entry level job.

Keith *"had a higher level of expectation of what I wanted to do,"* and so declined offers to do security work. David wouldn't want to be a Walmart greeter in his home town, but he would if he moved elsewhere in the country where people didn't know him.

An entry level job may right for you; it depends on what you want from work.

A Final Word

Days that you work are the only days you have lived.

– Louis Charles Alfred de Musset

We need "useful work when we're older," as well as "dignity, money, [and] proper medical services," wrote Alex Comfort, the gerontologist who wrote *The Joy of Sex*. These are no different from what we've needed throughout our lives. There is no end to a meaningful life in which we develop and use our strengths and make a contribution.

We need to write a new equation that factors in income, a fitting way of life, an appreciation for all that we can offer—our expertise and life experience—in a respectful and inclusive environment in which employers aim to keep us on in a variety of non-traditional capacities.

Ten years from now we might not recognize the workplace, a landscape peppered with shades of grey. We'll have a flexible commitment to work, take longer holidays and unpaid time off to care for grandchildren or parents; contract our services to former employers; work on short-term projects in Canada or beyond our borders; choose work that has tangible results rather than feeds bureaucratic paper-mills; launch small businesses or transform hobbies into income-generating enterprises; capitalize on talents and experience gained over the decades or explore new interests, all while enjoying a sense of control over our work.

Life is a work in progress. It's random and messy, and in that messiness we search for options. Those options have roots in experience. At times, the experience we build our next career step on isn't the most obvious.

Activity

How much time would you like to work?

Which of these time commitments would you prefer to make for work?

___ I'm okay with working full-time
___ I want to work part-time or have flexible hours
___ I'd like to work seasonally
___ My employer calls me when they need extra staff, and I go in
___ I like to choose when I work
___ Other

Sandra Konrad

Activity

Why do you work?

Which of these reasons to work do you agree with?

___ I don't know how else to fill my day
___ I still have energy for work
___ I need the income
___ I want the challenge work gives
___ I want to keep the social relationships I have at work
___ I want money for extras
___ Retirement has never appealed to me
___ I can't imagine 20-some years of retirement
___ Work is who I am
___ My work makes me feel important
___ Work helps to structure my day
___ I like the routine of going to work every day
___ I feel like I'm a part of something important at work
___ I am fascinated by my work
___ I want to work for myself
___ I've always wanted to…. I need to do it before it's too late
___ I can use my skills and talents at work
___ I need the health benefits
___ I like to earn money, have an income
___ At work I'm with people
___ I have kids / grandkids to support
___ I feel useful at work
___ I need to save more for retirement
___ I have to work a few more years to get full pension
___ I can't retire until a big project is finished
___ They can't get anyone to replace me

Review the reasons you've checked and put them into these three categories: current financial need, future financial security, and social and psychological fulfillment. A reason can go in more than one category.

Nine

Bringing Experience to Work

The compensation of growing old, Peter Walsh thought, coming out of Regent's Park, and holding his hat in hand, was simply this: that the passions remain as strong as ever, but one had gained—at last—the power which adds the supreme flavour to existence—the power of taking hold of experience, of turning it round, slowly, in the light.

– Mrs. Dalloway, Virginia Woolf

"And I don't know what's going to happen tomorrow," Maggie Muggins chirped at the end of each episode of the 1950s children's radio program, *Maggie Muggins*, that I faithfully listened to when I was a child. Although her adventures are long gone from my memory, her words still echo in me. Many things have influenced and shaped my choices, but her motto in part explains my openness to the career changes I've made. I've always wanted to be curious about what adventure tomorrow may bring.

The Richness of Experience

Experiences in our past, whether seemingly inconsequential such as that radio program or large, extensive behaviours or pivotal events, shape how we express ourselves and even underpin how we approach work. It is past experiences, as much as anything else, that explain why many boomers are ready to do something new. Having grown up in a time of rapid social change, today we want to learn and grow and be challenged.

Our experience is a rich resource filled with self-knowledge and ideas to inspire and help us build a new step in our career. Our accumulated knowledge goes far beyond the formal education and training we've acquired, and our experience, whether it's diverse or concentrated in a particular field, encompasses far more than the work we've done. We have developed skills and talents through work, hobbies, community involvement, interests, and that hard-knocks teacher, life itself.

In this chapter you'll read about boomers who built on elements of their past to create new work, whether they continued in the role of employee or became self-employed, a politician or even a student. You'll see how different paths might be presented to us, and have the opportunity to reflect on what might be sitting on your path, directly in front of you.

Tied Down or Move On

Life is a parade of tangible things and experiences we're drawn toward and others we no longer want and push away from. A sudden ending, growing dissatisfaction, a dream…they're catalysts that can launch us onto an entirely new path in our career.

Stephen summed up the push-away urge and the need to monitor our response to it. "I think a lot of people get to the point where they've had enough, but yet they're sort of trapped because of all these external factors, environmental factors, and they can't get out. So they keep plugging along. I saw that [it was time for me to leave] for sure. I saw it because it's my nature to be sort of self-reflective. I'm very introspective about things, and I think a lot about things most people don't think about. These things were creeping into my consciousness. A lot of times I wonder why I'm doing what I'm doing when I don't even like it, or it doesn't make any sense, but I keep doing it. Then I say, 'I'm going to take control of myself and stop doing it.'"

We might push away from the workplace that has changed. New policies, a new boss or new business strategies may leave us feeling we no longer fit, and that we don't want to change ourselves to fit.

We might push away because we have changed. *When Keith realized at age 50 that police work, with its physical demands and shift work, was a young man's job and that there were no positions for older officers to segue to, he began to wonder what was next. An opportunity to teach firearms at the police college in eastern Ontario helped him to see that there might be other possibilities.*

Stephen referred to being trapped in a job that no longer fits, but traps are extensions of ties that bind us to a job. Ties, or commitments, are necessary—we want the security of knowing how long a job will last; hiring agents ask what we want to be doing in five years. But we can feel tied so tight to work that our energy and spirit are constricted, leaving us unable to move.

The Ties that Bind

Three distinct commitments tie us to work.

The first tie is commitment to an organization's values. *Susan had long felt committed to the policies she wrote that underpinned programs for persons with disabilities, and to the government that supported her to do it. Over time she saw that her view and values no longer meshed with corporate values, and she began to feel that she herself was no longer valued, a situation that ate away at her passion for her work. Under constant stress, Susan lost the ability to think straight, the resiliency to adapt to work's ever-changing demands, and, she realized, she was losing the ability to hope. She decided that if she was going to put in 12-hour days, she had to do something consistent with her values. Two years after she quit her government job, Susan said, "We tend to think we have to grind it out, have less time to work things out for the future, and who's going to hire a 60-year old. You have to stand back from an unhappy situation and believe you have choices. We all know about the person who had a heart attack or a stroke, who was just going to hang on one more year. Or they retired six months ago and now are dying of cancer. We can't predict the future; we have to see that every day is important." She called it a trade-off. "Would I rather work 10 more years at what I like and earn less, or hang on to something for two more years and hate it? It's time to cut the cord and do something else, but there's a price to pay." Her decision to quit a year short of full pension didn't come easily. Two years later she said, "I'm always* amazed at people who stay at jobs they hate, because how would they get up and go to work every morning."

The second tie is the continuity or maintaining-the-status-quo commitment. If we feel tied by continuity, we compare the upsets and costs of leaving to the benefits of staying. In theory when the drawbacks outweigh the benefits, we quit, but many of us hold on to a hellish job for its few rewards if we imagine we'll be worse off if we quit. That is, more often it's imagined losses, not real losses that bind us, as well as an inability to imagine the gains of leaving. Fear can cloud our ability to predict actual losses, and fear of those imagined losses can cloud our capacity to put them in perspective or figure out how to manage them. When holding on becomes too painful, when it finally overpowers fear, we quit—although some put up with enormous mental pain before they leave. We hate to lose more than we want to win.

In corporate messages to employees, Carl heard constantly that, "Our people are our greatest asset," while observing that the same corporation was making deep cuts to its workforce. To him the corporation was making good business decisions but poor management ones. He watched the anguish of workmates who lost their jobs and wondered when his turn to be downsized would come. Although plagued by the lack of security, Carl hung on, tied to the future of retiring on full pension.

The third tie is the commitment of loyalty.

Rick had been working for 31 years when the business was sold to a new owner. This created the first crack in his loyalty to his employer, made worse because he and the new owner didn't see eye-to-eye. Had relations between the two been better, he might have transferred his loyalty to the new owner, but now Rick felt loyal only to the employees for whom he'd done payroll and solved problems. The kick in the pants he needed to move on came when he decided he'd done payroll long enough and saw no other job in the company to go to. Eventually he moved to a job in government and found that it's possible to trade an untenable situation for a baffling one. Two years on, he felt new drawbacks, but Rick didn't find them big enough to weaken his loyalty. "If a solution is logical, they [the bosses] do something different. If something has been working well for a while, they change it so it doesn't work anymore. Somebody makes a decision, 'This is what we're going to do.' We tell them it can't work. They say, 'You make it work.'" He managed his frustration by avoiding the office as much as possible.

Gerard's dedication to the job was only good for two weeks, between pays. "They're not dedicating anything to me; I'm only guaranteed to be there for two weeks. I can't make a decision to buy a new car that I'm going to pay off over the next five years knowing I'll have a job, because I don't know. The company doesn't guarantee you that."

The course of a career is a life-long wave with peaks and gullies. In a career and in every job within it we pass through three stages. The first stage is the engagement period when we spend time in preparation, in academic learning, apprenticeships and practicums. In the second stage, the mastery period, we deepen our skills and our understanding of our career's complexity. In the last stage, the disengagement period, we slowly or abruptly cut ties with it. In a new late-life career step, we'll go through the same stages, but we want a short preparation phase and we'll likely bring established work skills to preparation and mastery. We'll still want to deepen our skills and make a significant contribution in the mastery stage, but chances are we won't stay long and may disengage quickly.

We vary in our degree of comfort with change. Some deal with change if it's forced on them. Others accept change as a fact of life. Still others seek change.

"Those who tend to just see change as loss have a real hard time finding new pathways for themselves, whereas those who see gain in change can easily visualize next roles, next challenges, next steps, next opportunities, next alliances," said Kristen Cumming, who combines her knowledge of demographics and background in career development as a trainer, speaker and facilitator.

Underlying our approach to change are the commitments we make to our work, our employers and most importantly, to ourselves.

New Careers from Old Roots

Sometimes a job lands on your doorstep without you even looking for it, illustrating how organic and serendipitous a career path can be.

Keith's approach was to be open to the unknown. "Your perspective on life changes, year to year...I think you always have to look at other opportunities," he said. "You don't know what you're going to be offered. You never know what you're going to do."

Elle's stance was similar: "Be open to the opportunities. Look for the guideposts. There are things that come up any time in life and you think, 'I'd like to try that out,' but you don't do anything about it. I believe life is a path, with different doors that open, and you choose whether to go through a door or not. If you're looking for something different, you're more apt to see it when it crosses your path."

The 'what's next' step can be an extension of previous experience. But you might not choose to follow the most obvious experience, as the following people found.

Security work, a common retirement career for police officers, didn't interest Keith, nor did he want to wear a uniform any longer. In combination with policing, his decades of community volunteer work gave him a broad knowledge of his community, comfort in meeting conflict directly, and the ability to negotiate. Although he'd never been on city council, Keith entered city politics six months after he retired from the Thunder Bay Police Service. It felt like a natural step. "It was pretty scary, but I went into it knowing I was going to be mayor. That may sound arrogant, but I didn't enter to lose, and I was confident from Day One that I was going to get the job."

Driving vehicles into a mostly male-populated auction ring was "like being on a trip with my dad," Ruth said, recalling the closeness she felt as a child as she helped her father fix cars and farm machinery and drive lunch to farmhands in the field. The job was a far cry from the type of job she'd thought about before she retired, such as working in a dress shop or greenhouse, jobs which were extensions of her interests. When a former colleague told her about the driving job, she immediately said yes.

Selling war medals and memorabilia on-line was an off-shoot of Jim's post-war childhood in England, when he would pick up ammunition shells, pieces of airplanes and such while he played in fields, woods, and old air-raid shelters. He too had developed his interest alongside his father, who was renowned for his knowledge of military medals.

Ole grew up on the north end of Vancouver Island, and he'd harboured the desire to move back to a small coastal community for a long time. He and Karen had heard of the marina on BC's central coast, so when they sold their trucking business, they wrote the owner who suggested they take a look at the remote, tiny community so Karen could see if she could adjust to it. With trepidation she agreed to begin this new chapter in their lives. Ole started work at the marina immediately and Karen was employed shortly after.

As soon as she left the government, Susan began writing a book, a collection of stories of her experiences as a parent of a child with a disability and the experiences of families she had met throughout her career. The book helped her get her feet back on the ground and reaffirm her values and her passion after years of the thin-air work of writing policy. Her second step was taking a part-time contract position in a community organization serving people with disabilities.

Cora's love of reading and writing became the base for her on-line coaching business after she retired from teaching high school English. The business idea landed on her doorstep a year after she retired, when a friend's husband told her some employees in his company needed to improve their communication skills. Contracted by companies, she was soon teaching employees the skills to eliminate confusion in the emails and letters they wrote, and in the process, helping them eliminate a skill deficit that could stall their promotions.

Arlene's lifelong love of gardening was the root to her two endeavours. Winters and early springs she worked in a greenhouse, which added a social element to her week and gave her spending money. Summers, Arlene designed landscapes and operated a gardening business, of which she said, "People appreciate what I bring to the table. I work for satisfaction now, rather than hang in at a job I don't like just for the money."

Carl had intended to build a data wiring business after he left the telecom giant. It was good clean work and he was good at it. A year after retiring, he hadn't pushed himself to get contracts although there was work to be had. Data wiring had lost its appeal; he had to remind himself that being good at something and loving it aren't the same. Instead, he made a successful business out of his favourite pastime, renovating.

Childhood memories and experiences, hobbies and interests, and previous jobs gave these boomers a rich treasure trove to draw from as they moved forward. Each of us has such a trove upon which we can create new work. Tying fishing flies, cooking up jams and sauces, teaching an encyclopedia of skills, leading ghost tours—the list of new pursuits is rich and long.

We're Born to Learn

Growth is the only evidence of life.

JOHN HENRY CARDINAL NEWMAN, *APOLOGIA PRO VITA SUA*

Continuing to learn is crucial to aging successfully. We're either expanding or shrinking. We stagnate if we don't choose challenge, change and growth. If we try to remain the same, we fall backwards. That's true for both physical and mental abilities.

Not continuing to challenge our brain contributes to mental decline, and losing mental capacity is the change we fear the most. The adage "you can't teach an old dog new tricks" is based on our tendency to believe that we can no longer learn and a tendency to rely on old habits and what we already know. It's true that our brain processes information at a slower rate, and we don't perceive new information as accurately, as sharply or as strongly as when we were young. Too, our reaction times are slower, as is our working memory—we write to-do lists to compensate.

Put another way, the brain needs exercise, just as muscles do. It's designed for learning and it responds to novelty or newness, although not too much at one time. The brain can generate new capabilities; that is, it has the capacity to continue adapting to mental and physical challenges, an ability called neural plasticity, and research is showing that the brain continues to adapt—not decline—as we age. To maintain the brain's plasticity, its ability to adjust to new challenges and environments, the brain needs to be stimulated throughout life. We need new and novel tasks and to be engaged in mentally stimulating activities.

Bunny's motto was, "I need to learn something new every day or it's a wasted day. I don't know it all."

Cora liked to end online teaching sessions with clients by asking "What did you learn? What stands out?"

Lucky for us, there are two types of learning and three main ways to learn, so we have lots of options when we decide to learn something new.

Learning Skills and Procedures

To get in the frame of mind to learn something new, try re-learning something you haven't done for years, that you fear you can no longer do.

I challenged myself by choosing something physical I thought I could no longer do. At 63 I went skiing, convinced I'd lost the ability in the 20 years since I'd last skied and sure that no sooner was I standing on skis, I'd crash. The young woman fitting me with skis 40 centimetres shorter than I'd used in my forties said it's like riding a bicycle. When it was time to get off the chairlift, panic struck, but I pictured my choices: stay on the chair while it swung 'round to go back downhill or shriek at the attendant to stop the lift so I could get off. I was too vain to do either, so I plucked up my courage and snowplowed to a stop, breathed an apprehensive sigh, and snowplowed down the bunny slope at a snail's pace. The rental shop woman was right: what I knew about skiing had lingered in my body and mind.

That's an example of motor learning or nondeclarative memory, the ability to remember skills and procedures, such as playing a musical instrument or a sport. We need to engage our brain to make our body work in an intended way. I focused intently on my muscles' movements, flexing and tightening them as needed while breathing calmly. Two hours later I was planting my poles for parallel turns, though I was still on the bunny run. What else could I learn? I wondered.

Learning things we can speak about

The other type of memory is declarative, which encompasses remembering people, things, facts and places, things we can speak about. It employs different areas of the brain that nondeclarative learning.

SETTING OUT TO LEARN AFTER A BREAK

If we haven't made a point of engaging in a learning activity recently, we may find it difficult when we first set out. But just as starting small and persevering makes embarking on a physical exercise regime get easier over time, so too does continued effort with other learning projects. On the down side learning consumes energy and it's tiring, forcing us to deal with discomfort. And, some older learners may feel embarrassed if they struggle, while sitting amidst younger learners.

A number of learning activities turn on the control system for plasticity, such as learning a new language, learning to play a musical instrument, learning new physical activities that require concentration, and solving challenging puzzles. (We still won't be able to multi-task—if it was ever possible).

Exercising and sports, any physical activity, appear to protect the brain and even lead to lower incidences of Alzheimer's disease. In seniors' fitness classes, we move to '60s and '70s music while coordinating arms and feet in ever-changing patterns, a kind of learning that helps maintain physical coordination (which deteriorates with age), and the brain benefits because it must work to produce the moves. Stimulating brain exercises boost memory. Computer games help, not the ones we veg out on, but ones that challenge us to think. In all, we need variety.

GREY-HAIRS AT SCHOOL

We learn in three different ways, formally, informally and non-formally.

In formal learning, we intend to learn, usually in organized, structured settings such as school or courses, although it occurs in many settings. We typically compartmentalize formal learning to our first 25 years, so it's inspiring to hear of an older adult graduating university, though we suppose it's about accomplishing a lifelong dream, not preparing for a career change.

Going back to school to strengthen our career credentials forces us to master new skills and information. There are additional benefits: the learning environment broadens our range of contacts with the world, and we encounter new ideas, new people and even cultures—typically, we've specialized and narrowed those over the year, too—which puts us in the position of learning informally or incidentally.

Few of us pursue formal learning in our sixties for our career since we can't imagine a big enough financial gain from the money, time and effort we invest. However, if we engage in formal learning opportunities on the job, we tend to work longer, thereby increasing our income over time.

"You're never too old to go back to school," Julie said and then added, "Let me qualify that. After I finished the nurse practitioner (NP) program at 47, I thought I'd go into a masters because I love to teach. Today, at almost 60, for me to pursue a masters, I don't think I'd ever recoup the cost—courses are very expensive. Plus I'm working full-time and the energy is sometimes not there. I wish I'd continued on when I graduated from the NP program."

How much time would you invest? A year? Two years? One hundred hours? Regardless of the length of a formal program, you will burn the midnight oil doing between-class work. Fortunately, distance learning options are increasingly available.

At 60 Rhiannon began to study for a diploma as a career practitioner, much of which she could do online or in intensive, three- to five-day courses in two years. By her mid-sixties she had her optimal job of half-time work as a career adviser. She'd also liked the idea of doing research and so eyed a master's degree, but realized she'd need a PhD to do any significant work. She was confident she could do the work, but wasn't willing to study that many years. So after the diploma, she took courses to earn a certificate to teach Food Safe courses, work with roots in her food industry background and that offered abundant contract opportunities.

At 64, I completed a course to teach English as an Additional Language, a variation in my lifetime work in adult education and my passion to help newcomers adjust to life in Canada. I began to teach one full day and two evenings a week. My students came from many countries, expanding my cultural horizons, and I was struck by the admiration I had for them—they'd changed everything in their lives by coming to Canada. Especially, I stood in awe of older students—most hadn't sat in a classroom for decades—learning English.

The second way we learn is non-formally in short courses in non-formal settings, with no expectation of career advancement or certificates to tack to the wall. To enrich our lives we take language, cooking, craft or investment classes at night school, Tai Chi or Zumba class at the rec centre, a home reno' demonstration at a hardware store, a lecture about managing a medical condition at the hospital—the list is long. Instructors usually begin by asking students what they want to learn and then endeavour to tailor lessons to meet their needs.

Finally, we learn informally. We do it every day, figuring out how the new smartphone or navigation options on the car work; navigating the way to a new medical specialist's office; choosing the best features in new flooring or a hearing aid; how to cook more healthy food or sell your home…we set out to master competencies daily.

In all three ways we learn slowly, building upon what we already know and adding small bits incrementally. If learning is practical and fun, and we're learning something we want to learn, it's easier to stay motivated and keep on task.

If growth is achieved through learning, and learning is one of the strategies for aging successfully, then to add a twist to Cardinal Newman's words, growth gives us life.

Be Your Own Boss

> *Remember that not getting what you want is sometimes a wonderful stroke of luck.*
>
> THE DALAI LAMA

The Verger, a Somerset Maugham short story, tells about the verger, or caretaker, in a London church, a man getting on in years. Scandalous! say the vicar and church fathers when they discover he can't read and write, and let him go. On the way out of the church, the now unemployed verger stops to buy cigarettes but sees no tobacco shop. He decides to invest his life's savings in one. It prospers, and in time he has 10 shops. In 10 years he has thirty thousand pounds in the bank [it's 1929]. One day the tobacconist admits to his banker that he can neither read nor write. Astonished, the banker asks, "What would you be now if you had been able to?" "I'd be verger of St. Peter's," he answers.

Starting a small business is a growing trend among boomers. A 2004 CIBC report called the rise in small business owners among over-55s meteoric. Another CIBC report said that the over-55 age group makes up thirty percent of all small business owners in Canada and is a "key driver of small business growth."

Now sporting the moniker seniorpreneurs, we boomers turn to entrepreneurship more often than other age groups, in part because it's more difficult for us to land a job after losing one, but for many, operating their own business has been a dream. We want to be our own boss, to do more of what we love to do, and to be more flexible in our commitment to work to improve our work-life balance. Our experience, our knowledge of the area in which we create a business, our established networks, and a strong business climate can help us succeed.

Carl captured the intrinsic benefits of self-employment in his renovations business. "I'm doing it myself, getting rewards for it, doing it when I want to do it, and to my own standards." He was earning more than he did in his telecom job, and after a few years at it, contracts were finding him.

"Women Entrepreneurs: Leading the Charge", another CIBC small business study (2005), painted a colourful picture of the reasons women choose self-employment and the types of business they operate, which varied across Canada. At the time, women in Ontario chose self-employment to compensate for the lack of jobs; in Alberta women were lured by strong economic growth in the petroleum sector and its spin-offs; and in British Columbia, women tended to create business in international markets.

Self-employed women tend to be sole proprietors. Older female entrepreneurs want to balance work with interests such as travel and taking care of children, grandchildren or parents. But just as in paid employment, women business owners earn less than men, and, for the most part, don't earn enough to put money away for retirement, driving some to work longer.

The tough side of business

'Build it and they will come' may make an intriguing movie title but a poor business premise. Just ask the Dragons.

Less than five out of 10 businesses make it past their fifth year, for several key reasons. Often new owners don't know how to market their business and haven't developed a marketing plan, while a few people plunge money into a business without knowing if there's a market at all.

Determining the unique feature or service that a business will offer and figuring out how to attract buyers away from existing businesses or entice non-buyers to become buyers are critical. Failure often comes if new owners expect to make a profit much sooner than businesses actually do and don't finance their enterprise adequately at the outset. They fail to foresee the real cost of paying themselves for up to three years, the usual time it takes to comfortably pay staff, including the owner. Some end up financing their business on personal credit cards, which can contribute to a downfall.

As part of a marketing strategy, it's kosher to begin by approaching the people we know, not to buy our services or goods, but to be a source of referrals. Then push our comfort level to present our business to people we don't know.

Stephen's focus was clear when he began his consulting business, a professional executive coaching practice. He enrolled in an educational program to add a certificate to his broad experience, and shared his plan with his long-standing business network. By the end of the first week of school demand for his services, helping companies re-structure and down-size after consolidating, had gone crazy. In the midst of a contract he was too busy to do business development, so when one ended he had to hustle to get the next. "You have to work long hours and weekends if you expect to work full-time plus do business development," he concluded. After consulting for half a year, he took an offer of full-time work with a company he was contracted to. When he finished that work, he planned to go back to consulting, complete the certificate program, and get in touch with his network again.

Not knowing what is coming around the corner when you're self-employed can keep you alert, but it can also be stressful. In that regard, the security gap is narrowing between the self-employed and the employed: both feel the stress of not knowing if they'll have work tomorrow.

When Sally began her editing business, she had no idea that the search for contracts would be relentless. Often working seven days a week, she called her lifestyle "running on the spot to stay in one place". "I believe in following your own interests and living a lively and interesting life, and damn the consequences," she said, but the consequences—stress and living on the edge financially—weren't going away. The advantage for her was that she could combine her love of travel with editing from anywhere in the world.

Self-employment doesn't suit everyone. Being willing to chase down work, charge a good rate for it, and follow up on unpaid bills are crucial, and can feel daunting.

Linda tried to morph her hobbies—stained glass and fused glass, sewing, and wood carving—into income. But supplies were too expensive in relation to the income she would generate in Nova Scotia's local and tourist markets, so they remained hobbies.

"You'd think someone who taught economics and whose kids are business-oriented would have a little more business sense, but I don't," William said. "I make sure I cover my costs, although I forget to pursue a bill for an overdue rental at times. I [operate The Violin Doctor] to help people enjoy violin." His success came from enjoying his work, earning enough to pay one employee, and providing a niche service. His business might be more lucrative if he included crafting violins, but he didn't care to do so.

We might not assess our skills as something someone needs or would pay for. And we lack, or think we lack, the qualities that would make us successful.

Cora knew that 30 years of teaching high school English had given her skills that adults needed, but at first the only possibility she saw was teaching English to adults in night school at a local college. It came as a surprise when she found herself coaching employees, most often men, one at a time and online, a lucrative endeavour since their employers footed the bill.

David didn't consider himself to be a go-get-it kind of guy, which he'd need to be to get work. And PJ assessed herself as not disciplined enough to be self-employed and apt to undervalue her work.

With her long career in government developing policy, consulting might have been a predictable follow-up for Susan, but she felt no inclination to do so nor any passion to educate the public about how to access the services in the sector she knew inside-and-out.

A Last Word

We need faith in ourselves to face an uncertain future. It helps to believe that there is no such thing as failure. Each of us makes the best decisions we can with a stew of insufficient information, inadequate self-knowledge, and conflicting emotions. However, as we age, we know ourselves better and recognize our strengths and shortcomings that lead to success, and we are more sure of what we want from life.

"I've already created one life, so I know how to create another," Laura said about embarking on a new phase of her career in Canada.

Laura and others didn't recreate the life they'd had previously, but grew a new life on the bedrock of their experience. It was their dreams that gave them impetus and the hope to do so. In the next chapter we see how dreams continue to play an important role in our lives.

Ten

Our Dreams for Our Sixties

Nothing happens unless first a dream.

— Carl Sandburg

*"What am I going to be when I grow up?" It's a question
that really never goes away, because hopefully,
life is fun and creative and you never really grow up.*

— Bill Burnett

We all have dreams—wishes and hopes—for our lives, and it's common to put some dreams off until we retire.

Why talk about dreams in a book about work? I see three possible answers.

- One, our dream may be about our work—a dream to make a difference, to complete a project, to accomplish a goal.
- Two, we might work so we can afford non-work dreams.
- Three, we might need to juggle the demands of work with the pursuit of a dream.

In short, work can be the dream, an enabler to a dream, or a roadblock to a dream.

Building a Life on Dreams

Dreaming is a fundamental aspect of human nature that begins spontaneously at an early age, when something captures our spirit and imagination, and we say, "I'm going to do that."

We are inexplicably drawn to the thing that kindles a spark within us, the spark to know, discover, build, create and act, to experience a part of the world in our own way. The dream dwells within us, becoming a defining element of our lives. Both our ability to dream and our connection to our dreams endure throughout our lives. Unless, or until, we consciously do something to bring dreams to life, they linger within, waiting for us to make them come true.

Fulfilling our dreams is one of the critical tasks, if not the critical task we face in life. Unfortunately, we disregard dreams when we're shamed for having them as a child, when we're made responsible for others' needs instead of our own, when we're admonished to live responsibly, even told to get real. By late middle age, many of us have buried "impractical" or "irresponsible" dreams deep inside. But, it's possible to pursue dreams and be responsible. If dreams aren't the inspiration for our life, throughout life, we stall, tethered by "responsible" tasks and obligations, and fail to see that our ultimate responsibility is to lead a passionate life, pursuing the unfolding of our authentic self.

In our Third Age, work-related dreams may be long-held, once buried, or new.

I've Always Wanted to...

Do you say "I've always wanted to...."? Now, we see if we put off a dream until later, we might never accomplish it. We can imagine friends, gathered to mark our demise, saying with admiration, "He followed his dream to...." or "I'm glad she got a chance to...." or sadly murmuring, "He always wanted to...." "It's too bad she never got the chance to...."

In our sixties, the spark of buried dreams begins to glow once again. It's time to brush off the dust of neglect, the dirt of critical judgement and impossible thinking in order to see dreams for what they are—the seed of our spirit's desire. It's time to give dreams the attention they warrant, and to decide if and in what manner to follow them.

Gerard had neither accomplished his dream to become a teacher nor let it go; he talked about it somewhat wistfully during his last long stretch of unemployment. Married and father of two children who'd just graduated university, Gerard had never felt it was his time to get the education to be a teacher; besides, he had never been confident he could get a teaching job after he finished. He'd had offers to teach management courses at a technical college, as part-time contracts, that would have satisfied his dream, but he couldn't get time off his job to take them. So, his dream still lingered.

Perhaps you can't say whether you have a dream that's waiting to come true or what it might be. Perhaps you're living a life that is "as good as it gets". Dreams come, but they don't go away on their own. They fade, buried and forgotten, out of mental sight. Almost anything can revive them, but if not revived in the course of everyday life, they can be dug up. Digging them up requires that you give yourself time and permission to reflect on your past, as far back as your childhood and teenage years, to recall what inspired you or sparked your imagination then.

New Dreams

Dreams also pop up unexpectedly at any time throughout life.

A new dream flashed in Bev's fifties as she watched a friend cross a stage to receive a university degree. An instant realization: she wanted to cross a stage to get a degree, too! Somewhat later a serendipitous encounter led Bev to university. She met a recruitment officer from Royal Roads University and asked him about the possibility of becoming a student. He told her to send in her CV and other documents. Soon she was informed she could be admitted to the Master Program in Professional Communication, which surprised her since she had never earned an undergraduate degree. Distance learning made it all possible, and at 57, Bev walked across a stage to receive her degree. To fit studies into her already full life as mayor of Whitehorse, she got up at 5:30 every morning to study for two hours before she went to work. The next step: use her degree, perhaps consulting in communications.

Giving Dreams Life

Dreams are elemental and sensory, and lack form and specificity; those come later as we make plans to carry them out. A critical task is to identify the essence or heart of the dream. With that, we can set goals and plan steps to make the dream come true. The spirit of a dream remains constant although how to live it out can differ.

Julia's childhood inspiration to be a nurse in Africa morphed into something equally important to her, working in northern Canada after she retired at 65. As a nurse practitioner, she could see the need for preventative health care in communities devastated by addictions and high suicide rates, and anticipated working in six- to eight-week stints, a time commitment she thought would suit the energy level she might have then.

C. S. Lewis said, "Once a dream has become a fact I suppose it loses something. That isn't affections: we long and long for a thing and when it comes it turns out to be just a pleasant incident, very much like others."

Perhaps you've accomplished all of your dreams and don't have another in waiting. Again, dreams come unexpectedly. We hear someone's story, see a program on TV, find ourselves bored and decide to create something different…. Something touches our spirit and a new dream is born.

Roadblocks

Dreams come with roadblocks, more for some people than others. It's not unusual to think that pursuing your dream will hurt or inconvenience others, that others will oppose it, that you're too old for such nonsense, or that it's truly flaky, a pipe dream. Roadblocks are useful. They play the devil's advocate, pushing you to decide how important the dream is to you, testing your resolve, and challenging you to figure out ways to minimize or remove them.

Roadblocks come in the form of responsibilities, the constraints of money, age, time and health, as well as your own or others' judgement about a dream's practicality. Such constraints are based as much on limiting thoughts as they are on actual limits. We need to evaluate whether and in what way dreams can be realized.

We have four choices. One, we can pursue the dream as we always imagined it. Two, we can modify it and make it come true in a manner that fits our lives now, different than had we followed it earlier. Three, if we don't know how to act on a dream or have decided that it's not yet time to begin, we can put it back on the shelf until we're ready to look at it again. Finally, we can let a dream go.

Letting go of a dream means acknowledging that it was important and grieving (acknowledging the emotions of letting it go) its loss in order not to live with regret. However, if we feel our heart sink as we let a dream go or we notice that we've become cynical about our own or others' dreams, we need to re-evaluate in what way we can realize that dream. Letting a dream go creates an opening for a new dream to enter.

Dreams at Sixty-plus

*If they say I'm too old to do something,
I try to do it as soon as possible.*

— Pablo Picasso

"You're never too old to chase your dreams," said 64-year old Diana Nyad in 2013, after she stepped ashore in Key West, Florida after swimming 110 miles (177 km) across the Florida Straits from Havana, a feat that took 52 hours and 54 minutes. It was her fifth attempt—her first was 35 years earlier— as she navigated a course known for dangerous eddies, the Gulf Stream current, sharks, jelly fish, and shipping lanes.

Nyad, once the world's greatest long-distance swimmer, accomplished an extreme physical challenge at an age often thought of as too old to even attempt it. She had striven half a lifetime to achieve the dream, buoyed by her motto "Never, ever give up."

Long-held dreams lie dormant and re-emerge when life circumstances change.

Working in Africa was something Terri had wanted to do since her twenties, but her husband had never shared her dream. At 65 she wound up a three-year adjunct professor contract at UBC and then began to teach on-line courses from her Okanagan valley home. When she was 66 her husband died. Her dream re-surfaced, but now she worried that she was too old.

I told her about Audrey Griffiths, whose story I'd heard in the late 1980s. Griffiths, the grandmother of my then 11-year-old son's buddy, had just gone to Lesotho on a three-year contract with WUSC (World University Service of Canada), and was flying around the land-locked African nation delivering medical treatment in remote areas. Her husband had died at a similar age, and at 66 Griffiths was returning to the career she'd set aside to raise their children nearly 40 years earlier.

Our sixties give us distance from the demands of families and careers. Rather than being too old, this is the perfect age to dedicate ourselves to the dream, in whatever form fits now.

A Final Word

"When was the last time you did something for the first time?"

– Emirates Airline slogan

As Maggie Muggins' words inspire me, so does the Emirates Airline slogan. The movie, *The Bucket List*, spun an old tradition into a burgeoning trend—creating a list of things we've always wanted to do and places we've always wanted to go, and accomplishing as many as possible while we're still able.

We might list some nostalgic activities—visit the place we grew up in, the school we attended, the place our ancestors came from. But we're challenged to pursue always-wanted-to, first-time-ever experiences that stretch us beyond our comfort zone and make us do our utmost to achieve them.

Activity

Revisit your dreams

In this activity think of all your dreams, including work-related ones.

Your career map (the next activity) may show the road/s you didn't take, the dreams you didn't pursue. There are no should-haves, but you may have could-haves. Make your dreams more concrete by writing them down. How do you feel seeing them on the page?

If you're judging your dreams, talk about them with someone who won't judge you or your dreams. Ask for realistic feedback.

By acting on one dream, you likely move other dreams to the back burner. Turn your dream into an action plan; develop do-able steps to achieve it.

A dream asks that you believe in it, that you make it critical to your life. How do you feel about making a commitment to your dream? Perhaps you feel a certainty about its rightness, but a mixture of fear and excitement, too. As you begin to launch a dream, you may feel as if you're suspended in mid-air, as if you're a trapeze artist who has let go of one swing but not yet grasped the other.

Be bold; list your dreams.

Activity

Map your career – past, present and future

You have one career, the sum of your paid and unpaid work experiences. Just like geographical maps are drawn from actual exploration, a map of your career is a visual representation of the jobs, events, work-related and life skills you've explored. Making your career visual helps you appreciate your past and see where your career may be heading. Take about 45 minutes to draw your map.

Using a large sheet of paper draw a line, starting at what you consider the beginning of your career, perhaps your first job (delivering newspapers, shovelling snow, babysitting). Continue to the present, spreading the line across the page to include all paid and unpaid jobs and positions you've had. Include the dates you had them.

Mark significant events, such as courses, graduations, promotions, recognitions, and moments when you felt proud of your efforts and accomplishments.

When did you feel satisfaction in any of the jobs or positions? Try to recall what specifically you felt satisfied doing. "I liked that job" or "I liked meeting people" doesn't quite describe it. What specifically did you like about it? When did you experience flow? What specifically were you so involved doing that time stood still? Next, identify specific things you didn't like doing. Sketch all of these on your map.

Write on your map the skills you've developed that you prize.

Add the career aspirations and dreams you've had along the way, whether you acted on them or not. In *Working Identity: Unconventional Strategies for Reinventing Your Career*, Herminia Ibarra says that within us are possible selves, visions of ourselves that we have been, want to become, think we should become, or hope we never become. At a crossroads we often leave possible selves behind. Do you still think about one or two selves you left behind? Include them.

Extend your path into the future as you imagine it, to include the experiences you want to have—work, education and interests. Identify the skills you want to continue using and write them in the future section of the map. Include one or two possible selves you imagine in the future.

You may want to consider one or two possible selves as you establish a new stage in your career. Determine if you can use those prized skills in a possible self. Imagine yourself working in its environment, gather information about it, and try it out through volunteering, job shadowing, and taking practical courses. You want to make a good, logical choice that meshes with your vision of self.

There it is: your career path on paper.

- What are your first impressions? What does your map say to you?
- What sort of work do you see in your future?

Through such a process (there are others) you can visualize, plan and take the next step in your career.

Eleven

CHANNEL YOUR INNER WORKER

*It is necessary to work, if not from
inclination, at least from despair.
Everything considered, work is less boring than amusing oneself.*

CHARLES BAUDELAIRE

The plummy, part-time job I started when I turned 65 disappeared after two years when government cut funding. I had hoped to do it for a few more years. Again I had to ask myself, "What now?" Once more I had to get my head around having to work. Finding something I liked yet again was going to be challenging. Change is difficult, even when we want to change, and I wanted things to stay as they were.

Older workers in the 21st century face short-term jobs interspersed with lengthy searches for work. Behind each of us are health and financial crises, lousy decisions, screw-ups at work, all things in the past. We can do nothing about them, although they push many to keep working.

Feeling bummed out because we have to work or feeling discouraged when we have a hard time finding work are difficult places to be. We need resources—inner resources as much as outer types of support—to help us when one proverbial door closes and there doesn't appear to be another one opening.

Our inner resources are what we can control. Developing inner resources can unleash our inner worker.

I asked everyone for the advice they would give to the person who has to work but doesn't want to. Most people were reluctant to give advice. Some would say only how they had dealt with that issue; a few threw down a hard-nosed reality check. For the most part, their advice is about using the mind, our most powerful resource.

These are their suggestions. You may find some useful.

CHANGE YOUR LANGUAGE AND THOUGHTS

Our thoughts create how we feel. Change our thoughts and our feelings follow suit. The words we use also create our feelings. Using a negative word can make things feel worse than they are. Positive language can create more positive feelings.

Sally changed the words she used, which changed the way she thought about work, which in turn changed the way she felt. Instead of calling her work 'work,' she called it 'living.' "I need to go on living and doing things and trying stuff out," she said. She didn't struggle with the actual work of editing, but being self-employed came at a cost. It didn't reward her with employment benefits, and she felt at times like she was on the financial edge. As well, the need to always hustle up work felt a bit much at times, so she said yes to every project she was offered. Over time she widened her client base.

To help them feel free after decades of being driven by his job, Carl and Arlene were trying to put their lives ahead of making money. That seems to be a contradiction since they both worked full-out with their various enterprises. Carl recognized his need to keep busy, so 'keeping busy' was how he labelled what he was doing. Making money was a side benefit.

Rather than thinking of work as a burden or that it's unfair, we might think of it as an opportunity to set a new trend of working well in later life.

BELIEVE YOU ARE RESOURCEFUL

"You have to rev up your philosophy and deal with having to work if there's no way out," Sally said. "You've got to adapt yourself so you don't become crazy and

miserable. There are always ways out. You just have to be smart or work through it. We are very privileged people, with a lot of education and a lot of resources, and I don't understand how those wouldn't help you a bit, compared to somebody in a village in Africa. We have so many resources, so many possibilities."

"We tend to think we have to grind it out, have less time to work things out for the future, and who's going to hire a sixty-year old," Susan said. "You have to stand back from an unhappy situation and believe you have choices. We all know about the person who had a heart attack or a stroke, who was just going to hang on one more year. Or they retired six months ago and now are dying of cancer."

"Turning 60 changed a whole bunch of things," Jim said. "It gave me more of that 'I-don't-really-care' attitude. What can somebody do to me that's going to bother me that much? Do I care about losing a good job? No, because I'll find something else. I'm that kind of person."

"I was the professional, mixed-up student," Josée said. "I was emotionally fragile and that prevented me from being a success." In her early career she studied computer science, but by her fifties she had migrated to counselling psychology. Slowly Josée gained confidence and began to appreciate her broad experience and skills. At 69, she saw the coming year as one of transition, moving away from her work as a supervisor in a mental health clinic to teaching yoga.

I'm intrigued by an idea that describes why people build different sorts of careers. We're wired differently, says Emilie Wapnick in a 2015 TED Talk. Wapnick, who has a law degree from McGill University, is founder and creative director of Puttylike. Wapnick describes two types of people: specialists and "multipotentialites," a term she has coined. Specialists have one true calling and develop in-depth knowledge. Multipotentialites have a range of interests and jobs over their lifetime, and they develop a breadth of knowledge, become adaptable, and often apply knowledge from one field to another.

Both types are needed in today's work world. When innovation is increasingly critical to business success—survival isn't enough—specialists and multipotentialites each bring their strengths to teams in a "beautiful partnership" to envision and achieve what's needed next. So, whether you're a specialist or a multipotentialite, you'll likely continue to be so, and multipotentialites can quit thinking they went wrong somewhere and didn't discover their one true calling.

Set priorities
"We can't predict the future; we have to see that every day is important," said Susan. "Would I rather work 10 more years at what I like and earn less, or hang on to something for two more years and hate it?"

Be in for the long haul
To Lynne, embarking on a teaching career in her mid-fifties and having a hard time finding a job, having to work was about "...knowing and being grateful for what I have, instead of looking at the glass as half empty, seeing it as half full. Now, putting that philosophy into practice, getting on top of my emotions around things, feeling good for where I am and looking for the gratitude—that's a lot easier to say than do. It's not like I'm going to go hungry, but finding work might not happen in the time frame I want or need," she said.

Let anger and resentment go
"All the would'ves, could'ves, should'ves," said Arlene. "If somebody's going to spend any part of their retirement being bitter about things they missed, they need to move on, because it just makes you sick."

Constantly feeling angry affects our health and can shorten our life. It can also make happier people shy away from us. But more, we gain strength from managing the way we respond to misfortune.

Acknowledging the past is important, but dwelling there is unproductive and leads to depression. Drawing lessons from unfortunate circumstances helps to let them go. In my opinion, things don't happen for a reason. What's important is to draw lessons about how to manage ourselves in misfortunes and disaster, and how to straighten our world out again. Armed with such lessons, we can use our energy to create a better present and future.

Letting feelings of anger go is a process. The first step is to figure out what thoughts anger is based on. Thinking "it's not fair" to be let go, that our pension is lost, that we have to work, leads to feeling angry and resentful. It's true: life is not fair.

Ruth retired feeling resentful toward an administration she thought didn't care a whit for its teachers. She could justify the anger; after all, her health had been affected by working in a mold-ridden classroom that the administration failed to do anything about. She might have stayed angry, but she realized that being an angry old lady would compromise a good life, which was more important to her than harbouring resentment. She changed the thought that bred the anger. Instead of insisting they should have cared, she accepted that they hadn't, for whatever reasons. That allowed her to move beyond gut-eating resentment.

Letting go of unhappy feelings about the past may need to be done more than once. Each time anger about the past raises its head we need to again replace the thought that provokes anger with a more useful, but equally true, thought.

GET A GRIP
"Suck it up," said Don. "Heartless soul," scolded Gwen.

Yup. Sometimes sucking it up is all we can do. Accept that having to work is paying the piper—for having been a free spirit, for skipping school the day the lesson on saving for old age was taught, for changing jobs and employers, for leaving pension contributions behind…for any number of things.

Norm had come to terms with the fact that the paths he'd taken years earlier had been the best he could do. Norm worked, he said candidly, "to pay for my foolishness in my youth, the wreckage of my past." At one time he sold real estate, but his income disappeared after the housing market bottomed out. Then he entered insurance sales and pushed himself to succeed. "It was just go, go, go. The company wasn't talking about the quality of work you were doing, how you were feeling as a person. It was, why aren't you selling more? instead of what are you selling? Never how are you doing, and how are the people you're serving doing?" The work didn't suit Norm, and the pressure got to him. He quit, slid into an emotional trough, and didn't work for some time.

THINK AN ATTITUDE OF GRATITUDE
Don and Gwen both retired when they were 66, looking forward to having more time to look after their parents and to travel. They weren't travelling as much as they'd hoped, because at least several days a month and most months'-end, Gwen helped out in their son's business. Don and Gwen more than sucked it up. They were thankful they were able to support him.

Mary used a Buddhist daily practice of gratitude that gave her a sense of peace. "When I wake up in the morning, for about five minutes, I think 'Remember what you have. A good home, a good family, a beautiful house, all these skills that I can put to use.' Then I get up."

Look for the positives
"It's what you make of it," Norm said. He made a point of being cheerful to the grumpy old carpenter getting on his bus at five in the morning, the guy who didn't want to work at minus 40. Norm found positives in the fantastic mega-construction he saw going on in Fort McMurray and in meeting interesting people from all over Canada.

Driving high-end vehicles into the auction ring one day a week and the next day flipping burgers at the canteen showed Ruth a slice of life she hadn't experienced in the elementary school classroom. Watching people peel big bucks off thick rolls of money amused her.

"We need to realize what we'd be doing if we weren't working...sitting home and counting pennies," said Arlene.

If we only endure our job, we can try to work part-time, to make more time to do more enjoyable things, such as stimulating volunteer work or a satisfying hobby.

Invest in yourself and your career
Laura had already invested years in her career before coming to Canada. At first she found learning English challenging enough that she didn't mind stocking shelves. Two years later, she felt ready to get back on track in her career. She became more disciplined about being fluent in English, began to volunteer, and started to take health-related adult education courses in English.

Let the wake-up call motivate you
Breast cancer made Mary see that if she wanted to accomplish something, she had to get at it. "I'd been whacked in the side of the head. I'm mortal. I went out and bought that honking big leather La-Z-Boy couch and a 42-inch flat screen TV. [The cancer] gave me a new perspective on how I should live my life and what my

priorities should be. One of them was getting that book out." Besides working 30 hours a week producing communications tools for a federal government department, she was setting targets for her own work, writing 24 to 30 pages every three days.

News of Mary's breast cancer quickly spread to the people in our nation's capital who awarded contracts. Although she'd built a successful career and a company based on big communications jobs, suddenly all she got was a vague we'll keep you in mind when she submitted bids. "We've never missed a mortgage payment—that's sort of been my call," Mary said, when I asked if she had felt secure. At times the spectre of being on the street with a shopping cart full of her worldly possessions had been "a real motivator."

Stephen had saved and invested, following the best financial advice he could get, but the 2008 market crash gutted his nestegg, just as he was nearing his retirement goal. His decision to go back to work came after six months of retirement in 2011 during which he became increasingly bored. He also remembered the panic he felt after the crash, and still felt it from time to time. Knowing the market could crash again was a strong motivator.

Draw lessons from others' success

Other people's success, whether they've made success out of going back to work after retirement or never quit, are sources of inspiration and for tips about what you might do. It's one more time to think about the role models in your life.

C'est la vie and resilience

We need more than gritting our teeth and coping with uncertainty and things-gone-wrong. Obstacles and setbacks will always rear up on our career path. We begin by accepting that change is inevitable.

"The bankruptcies were companies my husband worked for while I was home looking after the kids," Linda said. "We had two different ones that went under, leaving us with humungous debts. We had to cash out all our RRSPs. Bad luck—it happens to everybody. C'est la vie. Life throws you a bunch of curves, and you just have to get through them."

"When I worked for the finance department, I screwed up in a big way," Doug said. "Nothing illegal or anything like that, but I was so embarrassed by it, I quit finance. I wasn't required to. Then, be damned if when I went into politics, I didn't let my mouth get away with me one time, and it was one of the reasons I never ran again. I had to recover from both of those. I have, or had then, a tendency to shoot off my mouth. I might have been a career politician if I'd been able to keep my mouth shut or at least my opinions to myself, when they weren't the most popular thing. But I've always been outspoken. I've just learned to temper it—somewhat."

Do We Have Choices?

A colleague asked, "What about people who have no choice? They have limited job opportunities and need the money. The lack of choice and the need to earn a living could be more strongly expressed. Are you saying, in fact urging, that actually everyone does have a choice?"

Several things lead us to think we don't have choices. First are the psychological ties to a situation you read about in chapter eight. Second is the flawed belief that if you leave a terrible situation, you'll jump from the frying pan into the fire. You might. I did, once, after not sufficiently researching the next job I took. But I jumped out before I was fried—had a heart attack—which I felt was not far off.

If you think there are no options, then there aren't. Put another way, you won't see options if you think there are none. I didn't see options when I quit, and had to remind myself they'd come.

We convince ourselves that we can put up with a not-so-good situation, and we can. But a bad situation tends to worsen, and as it does we ramp up our efforts to bear it. Meanwhile, stress accumulates. Eventually and usually, the situation becomes so bad that we're popped out of it—a heart event, an emotional meltdown, the sense that we're going crazy, or we become toxic at work and are forced to leave. The more intense is our stress, the less likely we are to see options or be able to think them through.

There may be nothing more painful than feeling there are no options. From all I've learned from others, I believe nearly all of us have choices. It's just that choices usually come with roadblocks and personal costs that we may not want to deal with.

A Final Word

*If you don't like what's happening in
your life, change your mind.*

– THE DALAI LAMA

To some, needing to work in our sixties and beyond may seem like an obstacle on the road to the good life. Channeling our resources—our experience, creativity, network, and the power of our mind—strengthens our inner worker, that part of our make-up that wants to contribute and do. With the support of others, the power of our mind can help push that barrier out of the way.

Twelve

WE BUILD OUR CAREER PATH AS WE TRAVEL

Years ago I was intrigued by the book title, *We Build the Road as We Travel*. The book tells about the development of cooperative enterprise in northern Spain, but I recognized the wisdom of the title as a fitting approach to life. Now, with as much as a quarter of our life stretching ahead of us, we can apply a similar concept to our career paths. The added years we will enjoy in our Third Age are uncharted territory; there is no roadmap. Since we will want or need to work, or both, we will need to construct our career path as we travel it.

Which Path Will You Build?

Long before our sixties, some of us might have predicted that we'd work until we were 70 or older, but I suspect most of us hadn't. Until recently, the good life meant full retirement at about 65, the age at which we'd take it easy, live on passive income, escape the rat race, and perhaps volunteer. In our sixties we stand at a crossroads, one road pointing to retirement, the other to work.

The decision to choose the path called retirement is so ingrained in our thoughts that it can feel scary, confusing, exciting and even exhilarating or a combination of emotions to choose the path called work. Neither choice is final. Ahead, the two paths may intersect. At any time we can choose to leave work and retire, and then leave retirement and go back to work.

We are changing our idea about what constitutes the good life. To be sure, some continue on the path of work because ensuring the good life means money to pay the bills. The good life may also mean making a bold move and starting your own business, enjoying a rich social network through work, engaging in work that challenges your mind and makes a difference, or structuring your day, month and year. Or any combination.

The Economic Landscape

Our career path will pass through an unpredictable economic landscape.

A lot has happened since I began to write this book. Another economic downturn has struck Canada, this time in Alberta, my home province, Saskatchewan, and Newfoundland and Labrador. Unemployment in the energy sector is wide-spread, a situation that, at its onset, was predicted to continue for up to five years. Homes will be lost, personal debt will sky-rocket, retirement savings will be ransacked, and people, including boomers, will wonder what they have to do to get a job. Prosperity can be short-lived.

Mandatory retirement in Canada has all but disappeared while we've matured, a significant change.

Some things have changed very little.

The Canada Pension Plan was improved to increase benefits, but front-end boomers won't see a bigger cheque. There continues to be a great deal of talk in the media about Canadians' meagre retirement savings, but in the 2015 election no political party offered a substantive solution to what is a growing social problem, aging Canadians with inadequate incomes. Fewer employees are able to sign on to defined benefit pension plans and are shuffled into defined contribution plans. Meanwhile, market vagaries continue to jeopardize retirement savings.

Imagine a Future

A few roadblocks related to aging and ageism need to be dismantled, so the career path stretching ahead can pass through friendlier territory. I imagine work has these characteristics in the future:

- Age doesn't automatically rule out being a contender for a job.
- Employers keep older workers on, no longer selectively laying us off.
- People intersperse periods of work and leisure more fluidly throughout their life. They no longer delay doing the things they've always wanted to do until retirement.
- Life-long work is valued, neither unusual nor in need of explanation.
- The term "senior citizen" no longer implies pasture-ready. It's time to retire that term. For that matter, there's no practical reason for cutesy names such as silver workers, the silver set, and seniorpreneurs, so lay off these words, too.
- Employment agencies and career professionals provide age-appropriate services to older workers.
- There are abundant jobs that respect the particular strengths of older workers and their desire to do meaningful work.
- A universal, adequate, pension plan exists that we all pay into, that provides a living pension, has automatic enrolment and no option to opt out or withdraw contributions early. Call them "defined ambition" pension plans that one can't fool with.
- Effective programs for saving for retirement reach more people.

Those are not too much to ask. Here's one last consideration.

The World Wants Us Working

The world is "elder-rich" today, says W.H. Thomas, in his 2004 book *What are Old People For?: How Elders Will Save the World.* He invites and challenges us to look at our aging selves in a positive light, calling it a "windfall", an unexpected good fortune of elders. We and all of society share the responsibility of channeling our strengths, talents, dreams and ambitions to serve not only ourselves, but society as well.

With a best-before date erased from our attitude, we can reinvent ourselves in our work and employ the resilience, skills and knowledge we've acquired in 60-some years of life.

We have a lot to offer. The generation that transformed careers from a one-job, one-organization, security-focused model to one of mobility and ladder climbing, has the wherewithal to explore and develop late-life work in its many forms. With retirement no longer a predictable life stage for many of us, we will make trade-offs in earnings, time allotted to work, location, autonomy, challenge and passion—to create a satisfactory career, with little certainty about how many more years we'll work.

Each of us is creating a road map of the future of work in later life. I hope you enjoy your path as it unfolds, with a light heart and a healthy step. I'd love to receive a postcard about your journey.

Activity

Set goals

*The man who moves a mountain begins
by carrying away small stones.*

— Confucius

What thing(s) have you always thought you'd do someday?

Dreams are realized by creating goals, by acting on small do-able steps put in order. No matter the goal, small, achievable steps and persistence are necessary to arrive at it. Generally, the step-by-step journey toward a goal is as satisfying as reaching it.

What things do you need to do in order to accomplish your dream? Brainstorm as many steps as you can think of—don't worry about whether they're in order or whether they're necessary in the long run—just jot them down. Then, start to create a detailed plan, by putting the steps in order.

A goal is **S.M.A.R.T.**
Specific
Measureable
Attainable
Realistic
And has a **T**ime frame.

Example of a financial goal

Dream: Have more money to spend on travel. Goal: Get a part-time job by (date). Save $(X) every month for (number) of months to go (where).

Goal: Be debt-free. Example: Pay off the credit card in 12 months from (date) by paying one-twelfth of the balance each month, and the remaining amount in the 13th month.

Epilogue

WHAT ARE THEY DOING NOW?

Stories for **Boomers at Work: Re/Working Retirement** were gathered from 2010 to 2013. Most of the people I talked to said they would keep working, so I wanted to know what they were doing three to six years later. Were they still working? Were they working as they had when we initially talked, or had they moved on to other work? Or, had they retired? Here are updates for most of the people you met in the book, sent to me in the fall of 2016. The pages on which parts of their stories appear are listed after their names so you can see a more complete picture of their career.

Barb: *57.*

Bev Buckway served one more term as mayor of Whitehorse. She wrote that she was "working as the Executive Director of the Association of Yukon Communities, utilizing both municipal experience and communication skills. Her volunteer work includes being Vice President of Vimy Heritage Housing Society, a non-profit organization that is spearheading a 75-unit seniors' supportive independent living facility, which will fill a housing gap in the Yukon for seniors who may not be able to manage their own house with the ongoing maintenance, but who are not ready for long-term care. The VHHS facility will be similar to accommodation found in other jurisdictions, with good company, two meals a day, and light housekeeping. If we need such a facility, then we future residents need to take steps to make sure it is available when we need alternative housing." *63, 70, 103,138.*

Bunny was in no big hurry to retire even after 40 years of service with the government and four in banking. She loves the new job she trained to do a couple of years ago after her old job disappeared, and finds it challenging with much to learn. She still enjoys her hobbies and especially being a grandmother and great-grandmother, but they wouldn't be enough to occupy or fulfill her if she retired. *38, 41, 43, 55, 76, 104, 112, 114, 128.*

Cora: With the recent downturn in the economy, Cora's 15-year old writing instruction business has slowed down considerably. She has noticed the loss of income which supplemented her pension, but with the increased free time has begun to teach a couple of three-month-long writing courses each year at a nearby university. Writing daily, she has compiled a family history, assisted her grandchildren to compose and publish their own stories, and written "what might be a final draft" of a novel. And, she is learning to play bridge. *17, 56, 62, 71, 78, 92, 110, 114, 126, 134.*

David: *39, 55, 77, 94, 111, 134.*

Don and Gwen: *24, 47, 71, 84, 102, 104, 149.*

Donald and Claire: *65.*

Doug Graham wrote just before the Yukon General Election was called. "Instead of gracefully retiring, as I said I would do, I've been convinced to run again in a different riding than I previously held. My wife and I have spent a lot of the past year renovating my old family home and we just moved in, after spending much more than we should have, but we love it and it has everything that the grandsons want, so they spend a great deal of time here with us. Still looking forward to retirement. Some day. Maybe." *41, 46, 65, 78, 80, 83, 92, 98, 102, 103, 152,*

Boomers at Work

Elle Andra-Warner wrote that even though her publishing company has done well, she's downsizing it to give her more time for her own writing and the things she "never has enough time to do." History appears to dominate her interests; she's director of a regional historical museum society and a regional transportation museum; she publishes projects about shipwrecks and lighthouses on Lake Superior; and she's involved in saving the icebreaker Alexander Henry from being scrapped. She's researching her family's genealogy and history, compiling a 'life box' to fill with memories, records of events and stories told her by her parents to write a memoir, a legacy for future generations. And, "I'm taking up one of the oldest hobbies in the world—knitting, once the domain of men." *46, 72, 74, 94, 107, 114, 115, 125.*

Gene retired at 70, according to plan. He hadn't sought part-time work, and was enjoying the leisure activities he found in retirement. *27, 38, 41, 43, 44, 46, 55, 73, 95, 98, 102.*

Gerard looked for his last job for two years before he was hired to a job a step down from his previous one. At 65, he'd held it for six years and had returned the money he'd withdrawn from RRSPs to support his family and himself during the two periods he was unemployed. He'd always defined himself by his work, but was facing an inevitable retirement, due to his wife's urging and a nagging feeling that he wasn't up to the pace anymore. *44, 124, 138.*

Graham: *30, 108.*

Helen: At 67 Helen quit trekking half way across Canada every winter to work. She also sold her house and moved into a small condo. *108.*

Jan wrote to say, "My father died at 96. During his final illness, we corrected the proofs of his last book together, and it was printed in time for him to hold a copy in his hands before he died. A year ago I moved to a flat, about half the size of my lower duplex, realizing that I needed less space now that my daughter lives in Europe. I turned 65 last fall and am now a pensioner, while continuing to work full-time. A small inheritance from my father has helped me get my financial affairs in better order. My living expenses are lower now and my cash flow is much improved. I am having the busiest work year I can remember, which is wonderful but somewhat stressful." Spending time with friends, and writing, in Tuscany is still a dream. *37, 42, 44, 47, 56, 60, 62, 74, 84, 93.*

Jim retired at 63 to a comfortable but not extravagant lifestyle. He still enjoys his life-long passion of treasure hunting, and it still yields an income, but he hasn't discovered the elusive Ugly Flower painting that would fetch him his fortune. *26, 43, 45, 46, 60, 62, 94, 95, 125, 147.*

Josée retired at 74, two years earlier than her mother had. She was making a successful transition to retirement, if retirement means teaching yoga more than half-time, in her own studio and at a seniors centre. *29, 40, 46, 48, 62, 83, 98, 147.*

Julie: *20, 43, 44, 60, 108, 109, 130, 139.*

Karen and Ole: Karen wrote, "I have been fully retired for 4 years and have two new bionic hips! Ole works part-time and plans to fully retire at the end of the year. This has given us more time away on our boat, which we hope to enjoy one more year here on BC's Central Coast. We celebrate our 13th year here in August 2016, and then look forward to going on road trips and camping with our family. We've had amazing and wonderful experiences up here on this coast, love all the friends we've made, and look forward to a new chapter in our lives." *30, 44, 52, 59, 72, 98, 102, 108, 125.*

Keith Hobbs wrote, "I'm in my sixth year as Mayor now and seeing great growth in the city. I ran on a platform of reducing crime and building a Healthy, Vibrant, Connected and Strong Community. Crime stats out last week put us #1 in Canada for crime reduction in several areas. A 30 percent reduction in youth violent crime really makes me smile." *57, 76, 77, 80, 84, 95, 98, 101, 102, 116, 122, 124, 125.*

Laura: *107, 116, 135, 150.*

Linda wrote, "Still working two jobs for five days a week…could work more if I wanted. My hobbies are still hobbies, and no plans to change anything in the near future." *39, 53, 65, 83, 90, 94, 99, 134, 151.*

Lynne wrote, "I felt like an ambulance chaser for several years. Five years later, with a full time continuing contract finally last year, I've found my 'home'. In the beginning it was a struggle to cobble together a full-time salary from five different sources of income. Now I feel settled and appreciated for all my life experience. I am the oldest teacher in the school, but there is a lot of respect given to me from teachers, parents and students. I feel happy and settled enough to stay here until I retire." *44, 111, 148.*

Marilyn: *31.*

Mary: *28, 48, 62, 63, 65, 70, 91, 103, 109, 114, 150, 151.*

Norm: *26, 42, 74, 80, 98, 101, 103, 107, 149, 150.*

PJ planned to retire from full-time work in December 2016. After a month's holiday—her longest in 30 years—she'll be available for part-time work for two or three years, where she's worked for the last 11. She's taken up Pickle-ball® to support her sister, who's going to the senior games in August 2016, and wants us to have a full team for the 2018 games. *30, 45, 52, 72, 95, 98, 99, 106, 110, 134.*

Rhiannon: *26, 40, 45, 54, 84, 106, 130.*

Rick: The month he turned 70, Rick retired from his job and started to withdraw from his RRSPs. That income and government pensions give him a comfortable income. *22, 80, 104, 106, 113, 114, 123.*

Ruth: *26, 42, 43, 52, 70, 98, 106, 125, 148, 150.*

Sally has found that, over time, her repeat clients have increased, and the pressure to pursue new contracts has lessened. *60, 62, 74, 105, 110, 114, 133, 146.*

Stephen wrote, "I have now been busy for nearly 4 years since I 'retired.' I learned that what I value is not uncommon in boomers. First, one must remain engaged in some way. It is invigorating and sustains you. Second, one must roll out of bed in the morning with a sense of purpose. To this end my wife also went back to work. I think a lot of people need a sense of purpose their entire life. It can be charity or community work, a hobby or a job, but to live a long life happily I think purpose is key. Finally, health. This is the baseline. Without it the outcome is obvious. More boomers are eating properly and working out than ever before—including me! One other thing I learned…I really am squeamish about drawing from our savings. It is not logical, because we saved for retirement. But now that I am there, we don't want to touch it! I've also learned that we are not alone in this." *22, 24, 47, 48, 62, 71, 94, 98, 114, 121, 133, 151.*

Susan: *44, 45, 52, 62, 84, 110, 122, 126, 134, 147, 148.*

Terri had found that the ability to work in countries where North American expertise is required is not as easy these days. The old, reliable organizations, CUSO, WUSC and others have many fewer openings. "I've applied for several things, but have only managed to go on three short-term trips to Peru where I taught sewing to a women's income-generating group. I'm finding my interests are changing, and I am trying to get used to my husband's retirement choice without him. I'm learning how to be responsible for my own decisions." *62, 100, 141.*

William continues to paint and had submitted two pieces to Sudbury's Galerie du Nouvel Ontario 2016 – 2017 season. The last violin he made in design, construction and finish, modelled after a 1686 Amati, was sold in 2014. (Its owner has won two fiddle contests with it). After 35 years as owner of The Violin Doctor he was about to sell his business. *45, 52, 93, 106, 134.*

Acknowledgements

I've always considered writing to be a solitary and lonely process. Yet at times, I've been overwhelmed by the fact that this work, especially, may be the authorship of one, but the product of many. My thanks for their contributions go to:

...the many boomers who honoured and humbled me by sharing their time and telling their stories. You gave me a full and rich picture of sixty-somethings at work in Canada today. I was heartened to find as much satisfaction and energy for work among you as I did, although not everyone felt such. I am inspired by your pluck, grit and creativity. I hope you find yourself accurately portrayed in the pages.

...MaryLeah deZwart, who with an eye for everything editorial—from substance to copy—and an ability to see the big picture, cleaned up a jumble of a manuscript lickety-split, arranging it in a more sensible order. Any shortcomings in Boomers at Work are my own.

...designer Marianne Unger of Mudstudio, Victoria, who asked all the right questions and gave me a cover with colour and style.

…Laura Kennedy, who translated my retirement income stool ideas to art, and snapped that photo as we explored Rome together.

…Jay McNaughton, my son, who coached me through the technical puzzle of designing my book's website and placed it online.

…the members of my long-standing Writers Guild of Alberta writers' critiquing circle who diligently read chapter upon re-written chapter over several years, encouraging me and making helpful suggestions as I struggled to say what was in my head and heart.

…the many friends who checked up on my progress from time to time and cheered me on.

…and you, the readers. I've sorted through a great many thoughts about my own career and the careers of Canadian boomers as I've written this book. I hope in some small way it helped you to make more sense of your career, too.

Appendix

KEEPING OLDER WORKERS AT WORK: HARD POLICIES AND SOFT PROGRAMS

As the population ages, Canada and other countries in the OECD share a similar problem: a workforce with low or obsolete skills, health problems and, at times, an abuse of early retirement, which is influenced by the way older workers are seen at work and by employers' reticence to invest in skills training for them, among other issues. In Canada, hard policies, such as changes to the Canada Pension Plan, will motivate older workers to keep working, but soft programs in the workplace will also be needed, such as age diversity training programs to moderate the prejudices about older workers and recast them as assets.

We can follow the lead other countries have established. In 2001 and 2002 the European Commission set a target to increase the average age of labour-market exit from 60 to 65, by 2010, in order to increase the EU's economic stability. It's been successful, although several countries suffered wide unemployment after the goal was set.

Finland was one of the first countries to develop strategies to keep older workers employed. Their older workers had low or obsolete skills, suffered more health problems, and were apt to retire early. It implemented pension reforms and training programs to increase aging workers' skills; adapted work environments to meet their needs; and launched campaigns to improve the public's opinion of older workers. It took 15 years to increase the average retirement age from 57 to just over 59. From 2000 to 2009 the number of 55 to 64-year olds in the workforce increased from 42 to 56 percent. An unanticipated benefit: their efficiency and motivation increased.

Employers, workers, governments and workers' groups all share the responsibility to ensure that the Canadian workforce is skilled. Canada ranks among the lowest of OECD countries in which employers finance any sort of training and education for employees, tending to provide training dollars to young workers. Older workers, in particular, shoulder most of the load for their own training.

Governments can take the lead in a partnership of those responsible for increasing older workers' employability by:

- identifying strategies to recruit older workers and keep them working;
- assisting employers to implement workplace age-friendly programs; and
- broadening the federal government's action plan, the Targeted Initiative for Older Workers, that aims to increase workers' employability by improving their skills level, in regions where work is scarce.

Canadian older workers and our economy would benefit from such a wide-ranging investment.

Resources

Chapter 1: Boomers Build a Long Career Path
Thomas Carlyle (1795 – 1881).

Chapter 2: Boomers and the New Look of Work
Action for Seniors report. Government of Canada, Fall 2014.

Baby Boomers Envision Their Retirement: An AARP Segmentation Analysis prepared by Roper Starch, February 1999.

James T. Bond and Ellen Galinsky. Context Matters: Insights about Older Workers from the National Study of the Changing Workforce. Center on Aging & Work/Workplace Flexibility. November 2005.

James T. Bond and Ellen Galinsky. The Diverse Employment Experiences of Older Men and Women in the Workforce. Families and Work Institute. November 2005.

Labour force survey estimates (LFS), by sex and detailed age group, Table 282-0002. Statistics Canada, January 2016.

Quality of Employment and Life Satisfaction: A Relationship that Matters for Older Workers, 2008. The Center on Aging & Work/Workplace Flexibility at Boston College.

Sharanjit Uppal. Labour market activity among seniors. Perspectives, Statistics Canada, July 2010. Catalogue no. 75-001-X.

Chapter 3: Show Me the Money

CIBC Poll: Most Canadians scrambling to find the money to make their planned RRSP contribution. newswire.ca, February 13, 2014. Economic Fact Sheet. Table 4: Proportion of labour force and paid workers covered by a registered pension plan, by sex, Canada, select year. Statistics Canada.

Peter Evans. Canadians' average debt load now up to $22,081, 3.6% rise since last year. CBC.ca/news/business December 7, 2016.

Paul Ferley, Nathan Janzen, and David Onyett-Jeffries. RRSP contributions 1968 to 2008… and beyond to 2020. Royal Bank of Canada, January 2010.

Global Investor Pulse: Canada. Black Rock Global Investor Pulse Survey.

How Canada Performs: Elderly Poverty. The Conference Board of Canada.

Jeremy Kronik and Alexandre Laurin, 2016. The Bigger Picture: How the Fourth Pillar Impacts Retirement Preparedness, Commentary No. 457. C.D. Howe Institute.

Rock Lefebvre, Elena Simonova, and Kevin Girdharry, 2011. Planning for Retirement – There is No Substitute. Certified General Accountants Association of Canada.

1952 – 1967 Reducing Poverty: What Canadians Received. Canadian Museum of History.

James Pierlot, 2008. A Pension in Every Pot: Better Pensions for More Canadians. C. D. Howe Institute.

Michael Prince. Fixing Our Pension Crisis. Lazarus Productions, 2010, vimeo.com

Sylvain Schetagne. Retirement Security for All. Lazarus Productions, 2010, vimeo.com

Sophia Harris. Seniors going bankrupt in soaring numbers: More Canadians are outliving their savings and spending their golden years in debt. CBC News / Business, June 30, 2015.

Richard Shillington, 2016. An Analysis of the Economic Circumstances of Canadian Seniors. The Broadbent Institute.

Monica Townson, 2009. A Stronger Foundation: Pension Reform and Old Age Security. Canadian Centre for Policy Alternatives.

Chapter 4: Sixty is the New…Sixty

Baby boomers: Can my eighties be like my fifties? 2005. M. Joanna Mellor, Helen Rehr, editors.

BBC World News, June 30, 2011, "Do people really want…?"

Sara Davidson, 2007. *Leap!: What Will We Do with the Rest of Our Lives?* Random House: New York.

A Portrait of Seniors in Canada. Statistics Canada.

Chapter 5: The Roof over Our Heads
Co-housing. The Canadian Co-Housing Network.

Charlie Gillis. Why Owning a Home is Bad for You. *Macleans*, September 29, 2013.

Global Age Friendly Cities: A Guide. Geneva: World Health Organization, 2007.

Kris Inwood and Sarah van Sligtenhorst, 2004. The social consequences of legal reform: women and property in a Canadian community. *Continuity and Change* 19(1), 1-33.

Diane Jermyn. One-size-fits-all no longer applies. *The Globe and Mail,* October 7, 2013.

John Bentley Mays. Boomers not opting for condos when they downsize. *The Globe and Mail*, Nov 11, 2010, updated Sept 6, 2012.

Luis Rodriguez. The Rise of Women's Role in Society: Impacts on Housing and Communities. Ottawa, Canada, February 4, 2012©

Chapter 6: Re/Working Retirement

Bad health is top reason for early retirement: Report. Benefits Canada, 2014, quoting The 2014 Sun Life Canadian Health Index conducted by Ipsos Reid.

BBC World News report that two out of ten people retire worldwide. 2010.

Building on Canada's Strong Retirement Readiness. McKinsey & Company. 2014.

Report on the Labour Force Participation of Seniors and Near Seniors, and Intergenerational Relations, October 2011, National Seniors Council, Government of Canada.

Retirement age of women. A report by the Vanier Institute of the Family.

Frank Tros. Flexibility and security for older workers: HRM arrangements in four European countries.

Chapter 7: Working for the Good Life and Chapter 8: Older Workers at Work

Bill Burnett, 2015. Designing Your Life. youtube.com.

CBC News online. Seniors' smartphone usage low among Canadians, January 21, 2014.

Mihaly Csikszentmihalyi, Feb 2004. Flow, the secret to happiness. TED2004. ted.com

Mihaly Csikszentmihalyi. Official website, Claremont Graduate School.

Anne-Marie Guillemard quoted in France's Labor Paradox. Bruce Crumley, TIME Magazine, March 14, 2011.

Diversity Talent Pool. Public Service Commission, Government of Nova Scotia.

The Age and Employment Network, cross-border information at taen.org.uk

Employment Insurance Compassionate care benefits. Service Canada, Government of Canada.

Lita Epstein, 2007. *Working After Retirement for Dummies.* Wiley Publishing, Inc. Hoboken, NJ.

50 + Works: A Guide for Older Jobseekers. Taen: Experts in Age and Employment. European Union, European Social Fund.

2007 General Social Survey, Statistics Canada.

Geoffrey Ford and Pamela Clayton, 2007. Improving Learning and Career Guidance for Older Adults: Good practice guide for career guidance practitioners, policymakers, social partners and employers. 2007.

Dan Gilbert, The Surprising science of happiness. What makes you happy playlist. www.ted.com

Jonathan Haidt. Beyond the book: How to Become Happier. happinesshypothesis.com

Nancy Irwin. ThirdQuarter e-newsletter, May 2013.

Janice Keefe. Supporting Caregivers and Caregiving in an Aging Canada. Institute for Research on Public Policy. Montreal. IRPP Study, No. 23, November 2011.

The Law of Compassionate Care Leave in Canada – 2014. Provisions by province and territory, Law Now 36(6) July/Aug 2014 p.1.

Matt Middlesworth, Ergonomics and the Aging Workforce. Ergonomics Plus.

Julia Moulden, 2011. *RIPE: Rich, Rewarding Work after Fifty - Your Guide to the Next Best Phase of Your Career.*

Bruce Newbold and Tyler Meredith. Where Will You Retire? Seniors' Migration within Canada and Implications for Policy. IRPP Study # 26, Nov 2012. Institute for Research on Public Policy.

M. Nurminen, C. Heathcote and B David. Working Life Expectancy Scale in Working life expectancies of aging Finnish workers in the municipal sector.

Responding to the needs of an aging workforce. An Aon White Paper. 2014.

Maire Sinha. Portrait of Caregivers, 2012. The 2012 General Social Survey. Statistics Canada.

Martin Seligman. The new era of positive psychology. TED2004.

Martin Seligman. Official website, University of Pennsylvania.

Staying Ahead of the Curve 2007: The AARP Work and Career Study, Highlights and Implications 2008. AARP Knowledge Management. Washington DC.

The Targeted Initiative for Older Workers (TIOW) helps unemployed workers, aged 55 to 64.

Third Age Guidance – TAG – Competence Coach. A PowerPoint presentation.

Working and Ageing: Emerging theories and empirical perspectives. 2010. European Centre for the Development of Vocational Training. Luxembourg: Publications Office of the European Union.

Chapter 9: Bringing Experience to Work

Dr. Audrey Griffiths. World University Service of Canada Annual Report, 2007 – 2008, p. 16.

Herminia Ibarra, 2003. *Working Identity: Unconventional Strategies for Reinventing Your Career*. Harvard Business School Press.

Staying Sharp: Successful Aging and the Brain. The Dana Foundation, 2015.

Emilie Wapnick, 2015. Why Some of Us Don't Have 1 True Calling. Ted.com

Chapter 10: Our Dreams for Our Sixties

Lizette Alvarez. Sharks Absent, Swimmer, 64, Strokes from Cuba to Florida. *The New York Times*, September 2, 2013.

Chapter 11: Channel Your Inner Worker

Charles Baudelaire (1821-1867).

The 14th Dalai Lama (1935 -).

Chapter 12: We Build Our Career Path as We Travel

D. Longino, 2005. The Future of Ageism: Baby Boomers at the Doorstep. *Generations* 29(3), 78-83.

Roy Morrison, 1989. *We Build the Road as We Travel.* New Society Publishers.

W. H. Thomas, 2004. *What are Old People For? How Elders Will Save the World.* VanderWyk & Burnham.

William Thomas, 2005. What Is Old Age For? *Yes! Magazine,* online.

Epilogue: What are They Doing Now?

Websites

Canadian Senior Cohousing canadianseniorcohousing.com
Ergonomics Plus www.ergo-plus.com
Emilie Wapnick's website puttylike.com
Martin Seligman authentichappiness.sas.upenn.edu/
The Canadian Co-Housing Network www.co-housing.ca
ThirdQuarter www.thirdquarter.ca

Made in the USA
Columbia, SC
30 July 2017